ramen remix

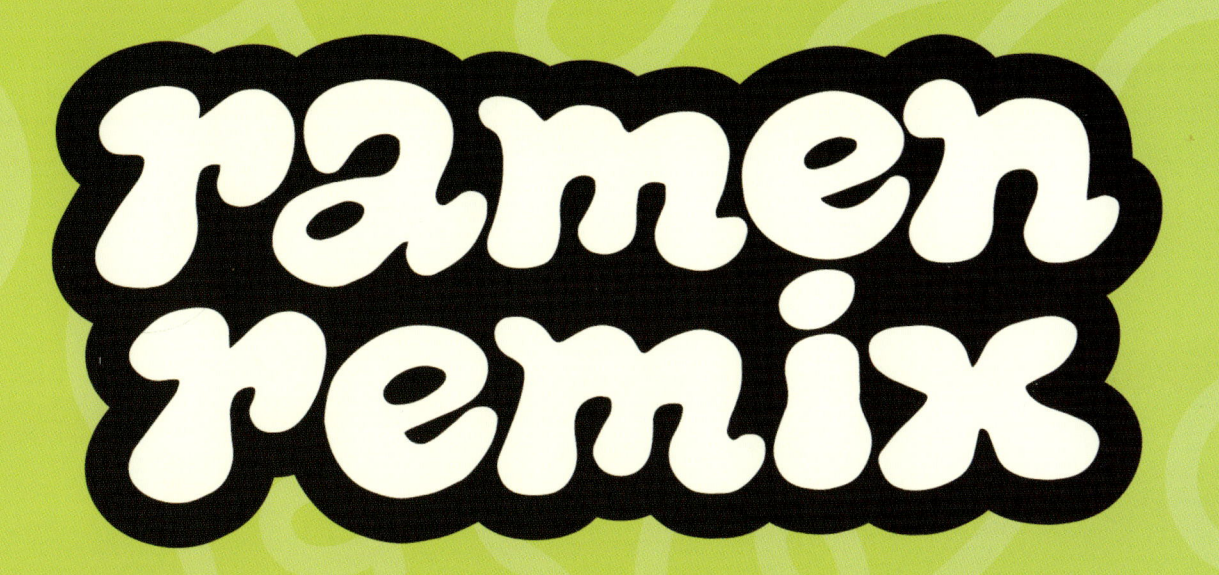

52 Recipes Using Everyone's Favorite Instant Noodle

Jessica Harlan

ULYSSES PRESS

**TO CHIP, THE SOUS CHEF IN MY KITCHEN AND IN MY LIFE,
AND
TO SADIE AND GILLIAN, THE BEST TASTE TESTERS
A COOK COULD EVER HOPE FOR.**

Text copyright © 2011, 2025 Jessica Harlan. All rights reserved. No part of this publication may be reproduced, stored in a retrieval system, or transmitted in any form or by any means, electronic, mechanical, photocopying, recording, or otherwise, except for brief quotations in reviews, educational works, or other uses permitted by copyright law.

Recipes in this book were previously published in *Ramen to the Rescue Cookbook*.

Published in 2025 by
ULYSSES PRESS
an imprint of The Stable Book Group
32 Court Street, Suite 2109
Brooklyn, NY 11201
www.ulyssespress.com

Library of Congress Control Number: 2025930803
ISBN: 978-1-64604-791-8
eISBN: 978-1-64604-794-9

Acquisitions editor: Keith Riegert
Managing editor: Claire Chun
Project editor: Kierra Sondereker
Proofreader: Margot Winton Parodi
Illustrations: Megan Badilla and Evan Wondolowski
Cover artwork: Megan Badilla
Design and production: The Collective Book Studio

Printed in the United States
10 9 8 7 6 5 4 3 2 1

IMPORTANT NOTE TO READERS: This book is independently authored and published and no sponsorship or endorsement of this book by, and no affiliation with, any trademarked brands or other products mentioned or pictured within is claimed or suggested. All trademarks that appear in ingredient lists and elsewhere in this book belong to their respective owners and are used here for informational purposes only. The author and publisher encourage readers to patronize the brands mentioned and pictured in this book.

INTRODUCTION 7
Ramen: A Brief Background 9
Ramen Soup Mini Recipes: 10 Easy Ways to Jazz Up Ramen 11
How Instant Ramen Is Made 12
Your Ramen Remix Pantry 13
Must-Have Kitchenware 18
Ramen Techniques 20

SNACKS AND STARTERS 23
Ramen Pan Pizza 24
Thai Basil Spring Rolls 26
Pan-Fried Scallion Pancake 28
Spicy Peanut Noodle Wraps 30
Creamy Miso Dip 32

BREAKFASTS 35
Bacon, Egg, and Noodle Scramble 36
Ramen-Quiles 38
Bird's Nests with Spinach, Egg, and Cheese 40
Ramen-Crusted Cinnamon French Toast 42
Ramen Brei 44

SOUPS 47
Asian Chicken Noodle Soup 48
Vietnamese Noodle Soup 50
Thai Coconut-Lemongrass Soup 52
Tomato Soup with Parmesan Ramen Croutons 54
Spicy Beef and Mushroom Stew 56

SALADS AND SIDES 59

Caesar Salad with Parmesan Ramen Croutons 60
Ramen-n-Cheese 62
Cold Noodle Salad with Grilled Beef 64
Chinese Chicken Salad 66
Southern-Style Slaw 68
Green Beans with Crunchy Sesame Ramen Topping 70
Spaetzle-Style Ramen Noodles 72
Ramen with Cherry Tomatoes and Mozzarella 74

ASIAN-INSPIRED CLASSICS 77

Pad Thai 78
Cold Sesame Noodles 80
Loaded Stir-Fry 82
Sesame-Crusted Tuna with Ponzu Glaze on Ramen Noodles 84
Sesame Chicken and Broccoli 86
Green Coconut Curry Shrimp Bowl 90
Dan Dan Noodles 92
Stir-Fried Vegetables in Coconut Ginger Sauce 94

HOME-STYLE COMFORT FOODS 97

Ramen Alfredo with Asparagus 98
Individual Turkey Meat Loaves with Crunchy Ramen Topping 100
Ramen-Crusted Chicken Fingers with Honey Mustard Sauce 102
Ramen Bolognese 104
Beef Stroganoff on Buttered Parsley Ramen Noodles 106
Kale-Cheddar Noodle Casserole 108
Zucchini Boats Filled with Ramen and Mushrooms 110

COOKING FOR COMPANY OR A CROWD 113
Soy Grilled Tofu on Gingery Noodles 116
Tempura Shrimp in Miso-Scallion Soup 118
Tuna Noodle Casserole 121
Salmon Croquettes with Creamy Chile Sauce 124
Salmon and Bok Choy in Parchment 126
Ramen Red 130
Ramen Mary 132

DESSERTS AND SWEETS 135
Ramen-Mallow Crispy Treats 136
Candied Ramen Sprinkle 138
Chocolate Peanut Haystacks 140
Ramen Noodle Pudding 142
Coconut-Lime Bars 144
Tropical Fruit Salad with Crispy Ramen-Coconut Topping 146

How to Poach a Chicken 148
Parmesan Ramen Croutons 149

Appendix 152
Recipe Index 156
Acknowledgments 159
About the Author 160

INTRODUCTION

INTRODUCTION

The mere mention of ramen noodles is sure to elicit nostalgia. Many people have memories of living on those little packages of noodles and powdered soup seasoning when they were in college or as they tried to make ends meet on an entry-level paycheck.

And indeed, for the budget conscious, packaged ramen noodles are the perfect food: They're cheap (my local supermarket sells six for $2), fast (the noodles cook in 3 minutes), and filling.

Admittedly, ramen soup, with its salty broth and freeze-dried vegetables, can get a little boring after a while. And certainly the sodium-laden seasoning packet isn't really that great for you . . . but that's where this book comes in. You can take advantage of the convenience, low price, and speedy cooking time of instant ramen noodles but use your own fresh ingredients, sauces, and seasonings to create a multitude of different dishes. Veggie-laden stir-fries, delicious soups, innovative appetizers, crisp salads, casseroles big enough to feed a crowd—all these and more can be made with those cheap little packages of ramen noodles.

And because the long, curly noodles are part of our collective culinary experience, a dish made with ramen noodles—especially when they're used in an unconventional way—is sure to be quite a conversation starter.

So stock up on those little packages, because with *Ramen Remix* in your hands, you're sure to find many more delicious uses for instant ramen noodles than you ever dreamed you would!

RAMEN: A BRIEF BACKGROUND

Although ramen noodles are typically thought of as a Japanese food, they actually have China to credit for their origin. After all, noodles and pasta originated in China thousands of years ago. According to one theory, in the early 1900s, Chinese cooks in a Tokyo restaurant created a brothy noodle soup called *shina soba*. Soba is a type of Asian noodle made with buckwheat, rather than the wheat flour that ramen noodles are made of. *Shina soba* became Japan's most popular Chinese dish and was served all over the country, with different regions incorporating local ingredients to make the recipe their own. Later, the name *ramen* was coined; it's the Japanese pronunciation of *lo mein*, the Chinese noodles.

In 1958, Momofuku Ando of Nissin Foods developed a chicken-flavored instant ramen noodle product in an effort to provide an easy-to-produce, convenient food option for citizens in postwar Japan, where food was scarce and finances were strained. At first, Ando's ramen was considered a luxury, since it was still more expensive for consumers than fresh Japanese udon noodles. But eventually people grew to appreciate the convenience, and soon other manufacturers of instant ramen noodles came on board with their own versions and flavors.

In the early 1970s, Ando developed another ramen innovation: packing the noodles in a polystyrene cup so they could cook in boiling water right in the package. The concept of instant ramen noodles spread worldwide, and several manufacturers opened factories in the United States, an ideal marketplace for a product of this kind, since Americans have such a need and appreciation for cheap, convenient food. Nissin's ramen, sold under the names Top Ramen and

Cup Noodles, is today one of the best-selling ramen brands in America, along with Maruchan, a brand started in California in 1977.

True ramen fans can visit the Momofuku Ando Instant Ramen Museum in Osaka, Japan. The museum includes a reproduction of the "research shack" where Ando perfected his recipe, as well as an exhibit of production methods, a display of ramen noodle products from around the world, a video of the manufacturing process, and a tasting room. There's also a hands-on workshop where you can try making your own instant ramen noodles, from stirring up the noodle dough to drying the noodles in the flash-fryer, and another interactive exhibit where you can make your own instant noodle cup.

Today, ramen noodles have shed their reputation as a cheap meal for starving college students (or the parents paying the tuition!). In the past decade, the number of ramen restaurants, particularly in urban areas, has skyrocketed, and there are even multiple national ramen chains. These restaurants often serve authentic ramen with long-simmered broth, fresh noodles, and a variety of ingredients. Supermarkets now offer a wider variety of packaged ramen, including gluten-free options made from rice or millet, and gourmet versions that mimic restaurant-style noodles, such as fresh offerings from Sun Noodle and Momofuku Noodles, developed by New York restauranteur David Chang, who helped popularize ramen in restaurants.

RAMEN SOUP MINI RECIPES: 10 EASY WAYS TO JAZZ UP RAMEN

When you feel like keeping it simple but still want to add some dimension to a bowl of ramen noodle soup, use one of these mini recipes to add just one or two ingredients to your dish.

1. Stir a handful of chopped scallions into the soup just before serving.

2. Sprinkle the soup with fresh cilantro or Thai basil leaves just before serving.

3. Stir in a dash of Sriracha, chili crisp, or other Asian hot sauce along with the ramen noodle seasoning packet.

4. Add ½ teaspoon toasted sesame oil to the broth and sprinkle with toasted sesame seeds.

5. Stir in a handful of chopped firm tofu or cooked chicken before serving.

6. Add about ½ cup frozen edamame or frozen chopped spinach to the boiling water along with the noodles.

7. After adding the seasoning packet to the cooked noodles and broth, stir in 1 lightly beaten egg until the egg cooks, then add a dash of soy sauce. Or, top with a chopped hard-boiled egg or a fried or poached egg.

8. Garnish the soup with a handful of mung beans or shredded cabbage and a squeeze of lime.

9. Sprinkle the soup with nori furikake (seaweed seasoning), to taste.

10. As the noodles cook, add sliced cremini mushrooms or reconstituted dried mushrooms, such as shiitake or oyster mushrooms, to the pot.

HOW INSTANT RAMEN IS MADE

Have you ever wondered how those little rectangular bricks of dry noodles are produced? A look at the manufacturing process is fascinating indeed, which might explain why the Maruchan factory was once featured on an episode of the Food Network show *Unwrapped*, hosted by Marc Summers. The ramen manufacturer Nongshim even hosts official factory tours.

At the beginning of the process, ramen is made similarly to any other noodle or pasta: flour, water, and other ingredients are mixed and kneaded in giant mixers, and then the dough is stretched into a thin sheet between two enormous rollers. As the dough is cut into thin, 100-foot strands, the noodles curl as they slowly exit the cutters. The noodles travel on a moving bed through a hot steam chamber where they cook for 1 minute. The steam-cooked noodles are cut into portions called *pillows*, then dipped into a deep-fryer where they cook briefly at 400°F to remove moisture so they're dry and shelf-stable. Then the noodle pillows are paired with a seasoning packet and packaged.

RAMEN ECONOMICS

In Thailand, sales of instant ramen noodles have been used as an economic indicator, dubbed the *Mama Noodles Index*. Skyrocketing sales of the country's best-selling instant ramen brand, Mama Noodles, accurately predicted a weakening economy.

YOUR RAMEN REMIX PANTRY

There are a number of pantry staples that you'll find yourself reaching for again and again to make these recipes. Here's a little explanation of some of the ingredients you'll find in this book.

COCONUT MILK Rich canned coconut milk is delicious in sweet and savory recipes. It comes in regular and light versions; the regular version, which contains much more fat, has a creamier mouthfeel and a slightly deeper flavor. But you can substitute the light version if you are trying to be healthier.

CURRY PASTE Jarred curry paste and a can of coconut milk is all you need to make Thai-style curries. Thai curry paste typically comes in red or green. One is not spicier than the other; instead, the red curry paste has a deeper, more roasted flavor, and the green curry paste has an earthier flavor. Try both to see which one you prefer.

FISH SAUCE This Thai condiment is made from fish (usually anchovies) that are fermented with salt and water. It is a clear, thin, salty liquid that is used to season soups and sauces. You can find vegetarian versions made from soy. The sauce will keep indefinitely in a cool, dry place. I prefer to keep mine in the refrigerator, although it isn't necessary.

GINGER Many of the Asian-influenced recipes in this book, particularly those in the Asian-Inspired Classics

> **NOODLE OF CHAMPIONS**
>
> Maruchan Ramen was the official soup of the 1984 Summer Olympics in Los Angeles.

chapter (page 77), rely on a hint of ginger to give them an authentic flavor. You can find fresh ginger root in the produce aisle at the grocery store. To use it, peel the brown skin with a paring knife or a vegetable peeler, then chop or finely grate the yellowish interior (a Microplane-type grater is perfect for this). Ginger that's grated, rather than chopped, will integrate better into the recipe, but even easier is to buy a jar of minced ginger, which you can find in the Asian foods section of the supermarket. It keeps for months in the refrigerator, so it's always on hand, and it saves you lots of work. The Ginger People (www.gingerpeople.com) have a version I like. Make sure to buy plain minced ginger, not pickled ginger. Jarred minced ginger can be used in any recipe in this book that calls for fresh grated or minced ginger.

HOISIN SAUCE Made with soybean paste and seasoned with sugar, garlic, and other spices, this thick, sticky glaze has a sweet taste and is great to add flavor and body to sauces or to use as a glaze, marinade, or dipping sauce. It comes in a jar and will keep for months in the refrigerator.

OIL Most of the recipes in this book call for either vegetable or canola oil (you can use the two interchangeably). Both of these oils have a neutral flavor and a high smoke point, which means that they won't burn when you're cooking at high temperatures, as you do for frying, sautéing, and stir-frying.

PONZU SAUCE This is like a tangier version of soy sauce; in fact, it is really just soy sauce with a citrus flavor. It makes a fantastic dipping sauce and can also add a salty tang to many dishes. You can even use it on its own to flavor a stir-fry or plain noodles.

RICE COOKING WINE This fermented, rice-based liquid has a slightly sweet flavor that adds a nice dimension to certain sauces and dishes. There are Chinese and Japanese versions; the Japanese rice wine is called *mirin*. It typically has a low alcohol content (8 to 13 percent). If you don't have any rice wine on hand, you can use dry sherry with similar results. If you prefer not to use alcohol, then use an equal amount of vegetable or chicken stock with a splash of rice vinegar.

RICE VINEGAR If you don't have a bottle of rice vinegar in your pantry, you're missing out. This clear vinegar is more subtly flavored than white wine vinegar and more complex than plain old distilled or cider vinegar. It makes a fantastic vinaigrette, and it's also nice splashed over steamed vegetables. In the Asian foods aisle, you'll see both plain or natural rice vinegar and seasoned rice vinegar. The seasoned version has added sugar and salt. I prefer the plain; you can always add a little sugar and salt if needed. Just make sure not to confuse rice vinegar with rice cooking wine, which contains alcohol and doesn't have the same tartness.

> ### RAMEN IN THE ARTS
>
> Instant ramen noodles are truly a part of American pop culture. Journalist Andy Raskin's 2010 memoir, *The Ramen King and I*, poses instant-ramen inventor Momofuku Ando as Raskin's idol while the author self-analyzes his failed love life. A 2008 film called *The Ramen Girl* stars Brittany Murphy as an American stranded in Japan who decides her purpose in life is to become a ramen chef.

SEAWEED SEASONING (NORI FURIKAKE) This sprinkle, which comes in a glass or plastic shaker, is a ubiquitous condiment on the table in Asian households and restaurants. It comes in several varieties but usually includes shredded dried seaweed, sesame seeds, salt, and sugar, as well as other flavorings like powdered wasabi or dried fish.

SESAME OIL Another classic Asian ingredient, sesame oil adds a delicious nuttiness to stir-fry sauces, soups, and other dishes. Toasted sesame oil has a more intense flavor. Buy the smallest bottle possible; you need only a teaspoon or so for most recipes (it's added more for flavor than for cooking), and this oil can go rancid quickly. For that reason, store it in a cool, dark cabinet, but not in the refrigerator.

SESAME SEEDS These are one of my favorite ways to add flavor, texture, and authenticity to Asian-style dishes, and you'll find them used in recipes throughout this book. Try to find sesame seeds that are already toasted, as they'll have the best flavor and a pretty, golden color. It's also wise to look for a source that sells them in bulk, such as a health food store, as they will be fresher and less expensive than if you buy the ones that come in little spice jars.

SOY SAUCE I use low-sodium soy sauce because I find that it's intensely flavorful without being overly salty. Choose an authentic Japanese brand if possible. Nearly universally, the low-sodium version is the one with the green label.

> **CELEBRATE RAMEN!**
>
> Happy birthday, ramen! August 25 is the birthday of instant ramen noodles. It was on this day in 1958 that chicken ramen by Nissin Foods was introduced.

SRIRACHA SAUCE This Thai chili sauce is a fantastic condiment for adding a little spice to many of the dishes in this book, as well as just in your day-to-day cooking. It's made with ground chiles, vinegar, garlic, and salt. Use it sparingly until you get a sense of how spicy it is; you can always add more to up the spice quotient of your dish. Keep the bottle in the refrigerator.

TERIYAKI SAUCE A sweet, thick, soy-based sauce, this sauce is delicious on noodles, or it can be used as a glaze for meats, tofu, or vegetables.

THAI CHILI SAUCE This flavorful Thai sauce is not superhot but adds a nice dimension of flavor. There's also a sweet version that has even less heat and adds a pleasant sweet note to a dish. The dishes in this book call for the regular Thai chili sauce, but you can use the sweet one if you prefer.

TOFU You'll find a wide variety of tofu textures, from silken, which is good for smoothies, to extra-firm, which can be cubed and used in stir-fries. There's also baked tofu, which has a superfirm, meaty texture and is usually flavored. I prefer the fresh tofu that is sold in the refrigerated section, but you can also find shelf-stable cartons of tofu that will keep longer in a pantry. To make extra-firm tofu even firmer for sautéing in a stir-fry, you can press the block of tofu under a weighted plate for 10 to 20 minutes to squeeze out some of its liquid.

> **OUT OF THIS WORLD RAMEN**
>
> In one year, Maruchan sells 81 million miles of noodles—enough noodles to extend from Earth to Mars and back again.

MUST-HAVE KITCHENWARE

To get the best results when making the recipes in this book, you'll need a few basic pieces of cooking equipment. Here are some of the cookware pieces and tools that I reach for again and again when I'm making ramen recipes.

CASSEROLE DISH Seek out a small covered casserole dish that is around 6 inches in diameter or holds 2 quarts of food. This is the ideal size for the smaller baked dishes. For the dishes in the Cooking for Company or a Crowd chapter (page 113), you will need a larger casserole dish, 9 x 13 inches. I like ceramic or Pyrex casseroles because they heat the food evenly, and they're usually attractive enough to bring to the table.

CUTTING BOARD A cutting board that is at least 12 inches square will be sufficient for chopping ingredients. I like wood or bamboo because they will not damage or dull your knife. If you cook with a lot of meat, you might want to consider investing in a set of plastic, color-coded cutting boards or mats so you are using a specific cutting board for each type of food (poultry, meat, fish, and vegetables). This will avoid cross-contamination and will help prevent bacteria from spreading.

FOOD PROCESSOR OR CHOPPER Several of these recipes call for crushed ramen to use as a crust or in place of bread crumbs. A food processor can pulverize ramen quickly and easily. You can also use a smaller food chopper, but you might have to work in batches if the entire package of ramen doesn't fit.

KNIVES A good-quality chef's knife and paring or utility knife are really all you need to make pretty much all these recipes. Be sure to keep them sharp, either with a home sharpener or by taking them regularly to a sharpening service—a dull knife can be dangerous.

SKILLET A medium (10-inch) nonstick skillet is ideal for making most of the 1- or 2-serving meals in this book. A small (8-inch) skillet is sometimes called for, as well as a large (12-inch) skillet. Try to find skillets that are ovenproof, as some of these recipes require finishing in the oven.

SMALL SAUCEPAN I find that a deep, 1-quart saucepan is the ideal size for boiling a single package of ramen noodles. A 2-quart saucepan is more versatile for cooking double batches or cooking the noodles and other ingredients all in one dish.

STRAINER A strainer is essential for rinsing ingredients and draining noodles. I like a small metal mesh strainer with raised feet so you can rest it on the bottom of the sink.

TONGS A set of tongs will be helpful for cooking meat, stir-frying, tossing salads, mixing noodles with sauces, or lifting noodles out of boiling water. Try to find a set that has silicone-covered tips so that it won't damage the surface of a nonstick pan.

WHISK A small whisk can be useful for mixing sauces and beating eggs.

> ### RAMEN WORKING OVERTIME
>
> Maruchan produces more than 3.6 billion packages of ramen noodle soup each year.

RAMEN TECHNIQUES

These are some of the techniques you'll see used in the recipes in this book.

HOW TO COOK RAMEN NOODLES Fill a small (about 1-quart) saucepan about two-thirds full with water over high heat. When the water comes to a boil, add the ramen cake (break the cake into smaller pieces if you want shorter noodles) and set a timer for 3 minutes, or according to the package directions. Use a spoon to submerge the noodles until they begin to soften and break apart. After 3 minutes, immediately drain the noodles. It's best to cook the noodles just before you will be using them, as they will stick together the longer they sit out. You can cook the noodles for a shorter amount of time if you want slightly firmer noodles.

CRUSHING RAMEN NOODLES When dry ramen noodles are being used as a topping or a mix-in, you can crush them by hand into small pieces. Place the cake of ramen in a bowl and break it apart into chunks. Working with one chunk at a time, use your fingers to break and crumble the dry noodles into the desired-size pieces.

> ### HUNGRY FOR RAMEN
>
> Vietnam consumes the most instant noodles of any nation in the world, with an average of 81 servings eaten per person per year, according to the World Instant Noodles Association. South Korea and Thailand are runners-up.

GRINDING RAMEN NOODLES Finely ground ramen noodles can be used in place of bread crumbs as a topping or in dishes. To grind ramen noodles, break the cake of dry noodles into about eight pieces into the bowl of a food processor. Pulse the processor 8 to 10 times, until the noodles are evenly ground into small particles that resemble oats, coarse cornmeal, or fine bread crumbs, depending on the recipe. If you don't have a food processor, you can place the broken cake of ramen noodles into a zip-top bag, seal the bag (squeezing all the air out first), and press a rolling pin over the noodles until they're crushed to a desired consistency.

When the urge to munch strikes, just reach for a package of ramen. You can really get creative with how you use the noodles to create a wide variety of tasty snacks and appetizers: pan-fry them into a pancake, roll them up in an edible wrapper, or bake them until they're satisfyingly crunchy. The snacks on the following pages can be noshed in the middle of the afternoon, passed around at a party, or served as an appetizer at a dinner party. So think outside the bowl and whip up some ramen-based snacks.

Snacks & Starters

RAMEN PAN PIZZA

SERVES 2

With its noodle crust, this is a fun riff on a deep-dish pizza. Get creative with all your favorite toppings, but be sure to have a fork handy, because this is one pizza you won't be able to easily eat with your hands! If you don't have an ovenproof skillet, transfer the noodles to a pie pan or a rimmed baking sheet after they've been browned on the stove. Top with the tomato sauce, cheese, and toppings, and then broil.

INGREDIENTS

2 (3-ounce) packages ramen noodles, any flavor
1 tablespoon extra-virgin olive oil, divided
1 teaspoon garlic powder
¾ cup canned spaghetti sauce or pizza sauce
¾ cup shredded mozzarella cheese
½ cup to ¾ cup toppings, such as sliced green bell peppers, black olives, pepperoni, or cooked sausage

1. Cook the ramen noodles in boiling water for 3 minutes, or according to the package instructions. (Save the ramen seasoning for another use or discard.) Drain the noodles, return to the pot, and toss with 1 teaspoon of the olive oil and the garlic powder to coat.

2. In a medium ovenproof nonstick or cast-iron skillet over medium-high heat, heat the remaining 2 teaspoons olive oil. Add the ramen noodles to the pan and use a spatula or a wooden spoon to spread the noodles evenly across the pan, pressing down to compress. Cook until the bottom is browned, 3 to 5 minutes.

3. Preheat the broiler. Remove the pan from the heat and evenly spread the tomato sauce over the noodle "crust." Sprinkle the mozzarella evenly over the pizza and add the toppings of your choice.

4. Place the pizza under the broiler until the cheese melts and the toppings are heated through, about 5 minutes.

5. Cut the pizza into wedges and serve immediately.

THAI BASIL SPRING ROLLS

MAKES 8 SPRING ROLLS

Noodles tossed with tangy rice vinegar and the fresh flavors of basil, lettuce, and cucumber fill these delicate rolls. If you'd like, tuck a few slices of cooked shrimp or seasoned tofu into each one. You can find the rice paper spring roll wrappers in the Asian section of your supermarket.

INGREDIENTS

- 2 (3-ounce) packages ramen noodles, any flavor
- 1 tablespoon rice vinegar
- 1 head butter lettuce, such as Bibb or Boston, torn into large pieces
- 16 fresh basil leaves
- ½ cucumber, peeled, seeded, and cut into 2-inch strips, about ½ inch wide
- 8 cooked shrimp, sliced, or 8 slices seasoned baked tofu (optional)
- 8 (8½-inch) sheets rice paper spring roll wrappers
- ½ cup hoisin sauce
- 1 tablespoon chopped roasted peanuts

1. Cook the ramen noodles in boiling water for 3 minutes, or according to the package directions (discard the ramen seasoning). Drain the noodles, rinse with cold water, and place in a medium bowl. Sprinkle the noodles with the rice vinegar and toss to coat evenly.

2. Set out the lettuce, basil, cucumber, and shrimp or tofu, if using, on the countertop, and have a clean work surface in front of you on which to assemble the spring rolls. Fill a shallow dish or a pie pan with warm water.

3. Immerse one spring roll wrapper in the warm water, holding it underneath the water with your fingertips until it is soft and flexible, 30 to 45 seconds. Lift the wrapper out of the water and hold it over the pan of water for a few seconds to let the water drip off. Lay the wrapper on the plate or cutting board.

4. Place about ¼ cup noodles, a piece of lettuce, 2 basil leaves, 3 to 4 strips cucumber, and a few slices of shrimp or tofu, if using, in the middle of the wrapper. Fold about 1 inch of two opposite sides over the filling. Then fold the bottom of the wrapper over the filling to form a rectangular pouch, almost like a business envelope. Tightly pull the top section of the wrapper toward you and roll it over the filling to overlap the other side, pressing slightly to seal the edges.

5. Repeat steps 3 and 4 with the remaining wrappers and ingredients.

6. Place the hoisin sauce in a small serving dish and sprinkle with peanuts. Serve the spring rolls with the hoisin sauce for dipping.

PAN-FRIED SCALLION PANCAKE

MAKES 1 (8- TO 10-INCH) PANCAKE, 1 TO 4 SERVINGS

This quick snack has an appealingly chewy-crunchy texture, and it's best eaten hot, as soon as possible after it comes out of the pan.

INGREDIENTS

1 (3-ounce) package ramen noodles, Soy Sauce Flavor flavor
3 scallions, light green part only, thinly sliced, divided
1 tablespoon vegetable oil
Soy sauce, for dipping

1. Cook the ramen noodles in boiling water for 3 minutes, or according to the package directions (reserve the ramen seasoning). Drain and return to the pot. Sprinkle the noodles with 1 teaspoon of the ramen seasoning (discard the remainder) and most of the scallions, reserving about 1 teaspoon of the scallions for garnish. Toss to coat evenly.

2. Spray a plate with cooking spray. Use clean hands or a spatula to spread the noodles out on the plate and form a flat pancake, about ¾ inch thick, pressing down to compress the noodles.

3. In a medium nonstick skillet over medium-high heat, heat the vegetable oil. When the oil is very hot, slide the pancake into the pan. Cook until the noodles are lightly browned on the underside, 3 to 4 minutes. Carefully flip the pancake over and cook until the second side is browned, about 3 minutes longer.

4. Transfer the pancake to a plate, cut into wedges with a knife or a pizza cutter, and serve immediately with a small dish of soy sauce sprinkled with the reserved scallions.

SPICY PEANUT NOODLE WRAPS

MAKES 2 WRAPS

This saucy wrap is inspired by a similar sandwich on the menu of one of my favorite restaurants, Highland Bakery in Atlanta, Georgia. The peanut noodles are on the spicy side, so if you have a sensitive palate, you can cut the amount of red pepper flakes in half.

INGREDIENTS

¼ cup smooth peanut butter
2 tablespoons rice vinegar
1 tablespoon soy sauce
1 tablespoon warm water
1 teaspoon sugar
½ teaspoon grated fresh ginger
½ teaspoon red pepper flakes (or to taste)
½ teaspoon sesame oil
1 (3-ounce) package ramen noodles, any flavor
1 scallion, dark green part only, thinly sliced
2 teaspoons sesame seeds
2 sandwich wraps or large flour tortillas
½ cup shredded lettuce, such as romaine

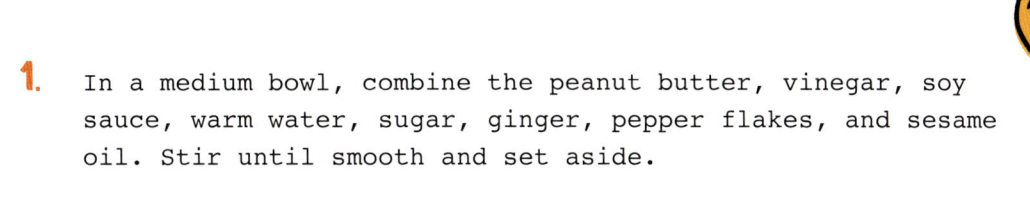

1. In a medium bowl, combine the peanut butter, vinegar, soy sauce, warm water, sugar, ginger, pepper flakes, and sesame oil. Stir until smooth and set aside.

2. Cook the ramen noodles in boiling water for 3 minutes, or according to the package directions (discard the ramen seasoning). Drain the noodles and return to the pot or place in a bowl.

3. Pour the peanut butter sauce over the noodles, sprinkle with the scallion and sesame seeds, and stir to combine. Sauced noodles can be kept covered in the refrigerator for 1 to 2 days.

4. Set the sandwich wraps on a clean work surface. Divide the sesame noodles between the wraps, mounding them in the center of each one. Place half the lettuce on each mound of noodles. Wrap the sandwich by folding two opposite sides of the wraps over the filling, then rolling the rest of the wrap around the filling from bottom to top. Cut each sandwich in half diagonally. Serve immediately.

CREAMY MISO DIP

MAKES ½ CUP

Many of the recipes in this book don't use the seasoning packet that comes with each package of ramen noodles, but this recipe gives you the chance to use some of those wasted packets. This dip is fantastic with celery and carrot sticks, or keep with the Asian theme and serve it with snow peas, bok choy stems, and red bell pepper spears.

INGREDIENTS

½ cup sour cream
1 packet ramen seasoning of your choice
   (save the noodles for another recipe)

1. In a small bowl, combine the sour cream and ramen seasoning and stir well. Cover with plastic wrap and refrigerate for at least 30 minutes to allow the flavors to meld.

> **VARIATION**
>
> For a healthier dip, substitute plain low-fat Greek-style yogurt for half of the sour cream.

Here in the United States, we tend to have a pretty strict definition of breakfast: eggs, pancakes, waffles, toast, cereal, maybe some smoked fish if we're feeling adventurous. But make room for noodles in your morning meal, whether they're incorporated into a traditional breakfast dish or a recipe that deliciously pushes the breakfast boundaries you're used to.

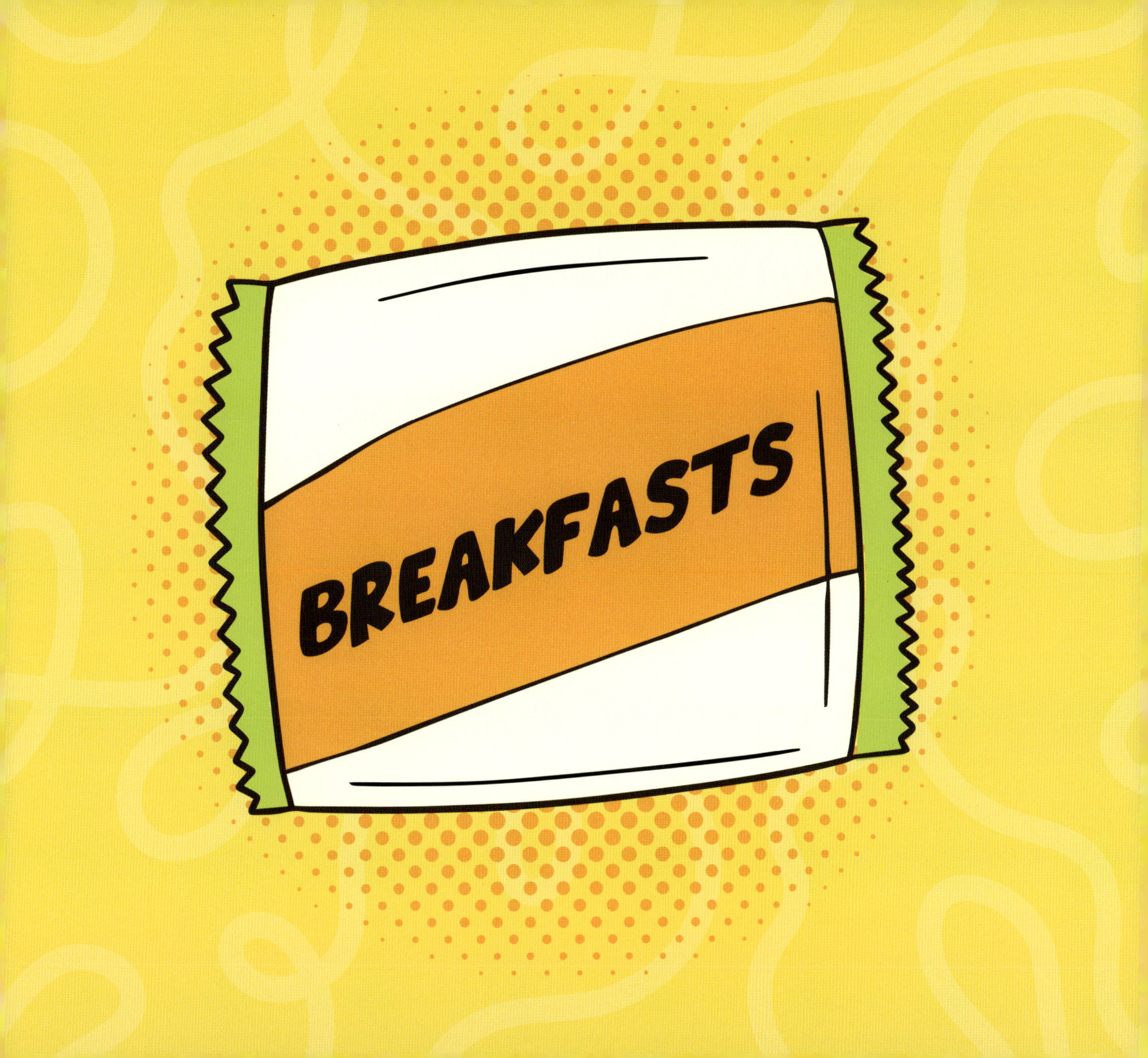
BREAKFASTS

BACON, EGG, AND NOODLE SCRAMBLE

SERVES 1

I love this quick, satisfying breakfast for one. It's fast to make and is an indulgent treat when it's just you and the Sunday paper. Add a cup of coffee and a wedge or two of cantaloupe, and you're set.

INGREDIENTS

1 (3-ounce) package ramen noodles, any flavor
2 strips bacon
½ tablespoon unsalted butter
2 large eggs
1 ounce Cheddar or Colby cheese, shredded (about 2 tablespoons)
Salt and pepper

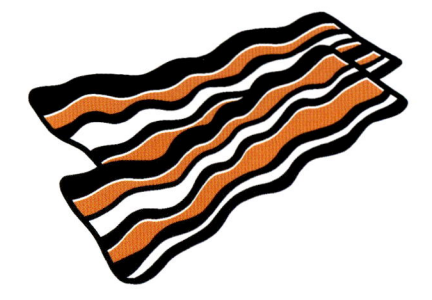

1. Break the cake of ramen noodles into about eight pieces and cook them in boiling water for 3 minutes, or according to the package directions (discard the ramen seasoning). Drain and set aside.

2. In a medium nonstick skillet over medium-high heat, cook the bacon until crisp, 7 to 10 minutes, turning over as needed to evenly cook both sides. Remove the bacon from the pan and drain any excess fat if necessary, so there's no more than about 1 teaspoon of bacon fat left. When the bacon cools, crumble it into pieces and set aside.

3. Add the butter to the hot pan with the bacon fat. When the butter melts, add the noodles and cook, stirring frequently, until lightly browned, 3 to 4 minutes. Meanwhile, beat the eggs lightly in a small bowl with a fork or a whisk. Turn down the heat to low and add the eggs to the pan. Cook, stirring, until the eggs are nearly scrambled, about 4 minutes. Sprinkle the cheese over the eggs and cook, stirring frequently, until the cheese melts.

4. Transfer to a plate or a shallow bowl, season to taste with salt and pepper, sprinkle the crumbled bacon on top, and serve.

RAMEN-QUILES

SERVES 2 TO 3

Chilaquiles is a popular Mexican breakfast dish that makes use of stale leftover tortillas. The tortilla pieces are fried in oil, then simmered in a tomato-chile sauce, like the sauce that is used on enchiladas. Here, I've used dry ramen noodles, which soften in the sauce. Use traditional Mexican toppings, like diced avocado, fresh cilantro, and queso fresco (a crumbly Mexican cheese that can be found in the ethnic section of most supermarkets or at a Mexican grocery). Serve this with scrambled eggs and refried beans for a hearty Mexican-style breakfast.

INGREDIENTS

1 (15-ounce) can tomato sauce or tomato puree
2 canned chipotle peppers in adobo sauce
½ teaspoon ground cumin
2 (3-ounce) packages ramen noodles, any flavor
1 tablespoon vegetable oil
1 small onion, diced
1 avocado, diced
2 tablespoons chopped fresh cilantro
1 ounce queso fresco, crumbled

1. In a blender or food processor, puree the tomato sauce, chipotle peppers, and cumin.

2. In a medium bowl, crumble the ramen noodles (discard the ramen seasoning).

3. In a medium saucepan over medium heat, heat the vegetable oil. Add the onion and the crumbled ramen noodles and sauté, stirring frequently, until the onion is softened and the ramen begins to brown, about 5 minutes.

4. Pour the tomato sauce over the noodles, stir to combine, and simmer over medium heat until the noodles are just softened but still have a firm texture, 4 to 5 minutes.

5. To serve, divide the noodles among two or three plates and top with the avocado, cilantro, and queso fresco.

BIRD'S NESTS WITH SPINACH, EGG, AND CHEESE

SERVES 2 TO 4

A fun option for a special brunch or breakfast, these little noodle nests are made in muffin pans and filled with baked eggs. Two of these nests will make a substantial breakfast; at a brunch where you're serving other dishes, you can allow one bird's nest per person.

INGREDIENTS

1 (3-ounce) package ramen noodles, chicken flavor
1 teaspoon sesame oil
½ cup thawed frozen spinach, excess water squeezed out
4 large eggs
¼ cup shredded Colby or Cheddar cheese
Salt and pepper

1. Preheat the oven to 350°F. Spray 4 cups of a standard muffin pan with cooking spray.

2. Cook the ramen noodles in boiling water for 3 minutes, or according to the package directions (reserve the ramen seasoning). Drain the noodles, return them to the pot, and toss with ½ teaspoon of the ramen seasoning (discard the remainder) and the sesame oil.

3. When the noodles are cool enough to handle, press the noodles into the prepared muffin cups, pressing against the bottom and sides of the pan to form a bowl shape that resembles a bird's nest. Bake until the edges turn brown and the noodles begin to harden and turn crisp on the bottom and sides, 20 to 25 minutes. Remove from the oven.

4. Fill each nest with about 2 tablespoons spinach. Being careful to keep the yolk intact, break 1 egg into each nest over the spinach. Return the pan to the oven and bake until the egg white is solid but the yolk still feels liquid, 10 to 12 minutes. Sprinkle each bird's nest with shredded cheese (about 1 tablespoon each) and bake for 1 minute more. Season to taste with salt and pepper and serve immediately.

RAMEN-CRUSTED CINNAMON FRENCH TOAST

SERVES 4

My kids beg for seconds of this version of French toast, which gets a little crunch from a coating of sweetened dry ramen noodles, when I make it for them on the weekends. This dish is great with maple syrup, but try it with fruit sauce instead for a twist. Bread that's slightly stale makes the best French toast because it's dried out enough to absorb the egg custard. If your bread is still moist, you could put it in a warm (200°F) oven until the center of the bread starts to dry out a little, 5 to 10 minutes.

INGREDIENTS

- 1 tablespoon unsalted butter, plus more for cooking
- 1 teaspoon sugar
- 1½ teaspoons ground cinnamon, divided
- 1 (3-ounce) package ramen noodles, any flavor
- 4 large eggs
- ¼ cup half-and-half or whole milk
- 1 teaspoon vanilla extract
- Pinch of salt
- 8 slices day-old crusty bread, such as baguette

1. In a small nonstick skillet, melt 1 tablespoon of the butter. Sprinkle the sugar and 1 teaspoon of the cinnamon into the pan and stir to melt the sugar. Crumble the ramen noodles into the pan and cook, stirring constantly, until the noodles are completely coated with the sugar mixture and golden brown, about 5 minutes (discard the ramen seasoning).

2. Transfer the ramen to a food processor and pulse until finely ground. Spread the ramen mixture in a shallow dish, such as a pie pan.

3. In a medium bowl, whisk together the eggs, half-and-half or milk, vanilla, remaining ½ teaspoon cinnamon, and salt.

4. Heat a griddle or a large skillet over medium-high heat. Coat the cooking surface lightly with butter.

5. Dip one slice of bread into the egg mixture, hold it over the bowl to let the excess drip off, then set the bread in the ramen mixture to coat it completely, pressing the ramen noodles into the bread to make them stick. Repeat with the remaining bread slices. Working in batches if necessary, put the crusted French toast on the hot griddle or skillet and cook until browned, about 4 minutes on each side. Serve immediately.

RAMEN BREI

SERVES 2

Jewish people often make a breakfast dish called matzoh brei from the unleavened cracker-bread eaten during the Passover holiday. Moistened matzoh is scrambled with eggs and served either sprinkled with salt and pepper or sweetened with maple syrup, and uncooked ramen noodles can be used in the same way. If you'd like to try it savory, omit the cinnamon and serve your ramen brei with salt and pepper and maybe a dash of hot sauce.

INGREDIENTS

1 (3-ounce) package ramen noodles, any flavor
¾ cup milk
2 large eggs
½ teaspoon ground cinnamon
1 tablespoon unsalted butter
Maple syrup, to serve

1. In a small bowl, break the ramen noodles into bite-size chunks (discard the ramen seasoning). Pour the milk over the noodles so they are nearly completely covered and let sit, stirring occasionally, for 10 minutes.

2. Break the eggs into a second small bowl and whisk until smooth. Add the cinnamon and stir to combine.

3. In a small nonstick skillet over medium-high heat, melt the butter, tilting to coat the bottom of the pan. Drain the excess milk from the ramen noodles and add them to the pan. Add the eggs and cook, stirring constantly with a rubber spatula, until the eggs are completely cooked and the ramen is lightly browned, about 5 minutes. Serve hot, drizzled with maple syrup or pancake syrup.

Ramen noodles are at their most traditional when swimming in a flavorful soup—but that doesn't mean you can't have fun and get creative. After all, think of all the classic soup recipes around the world that include noodles, from chicken noodle to minestrone. On a chilly night, brew up one of these satisfying recipes for an easy, warming supper.

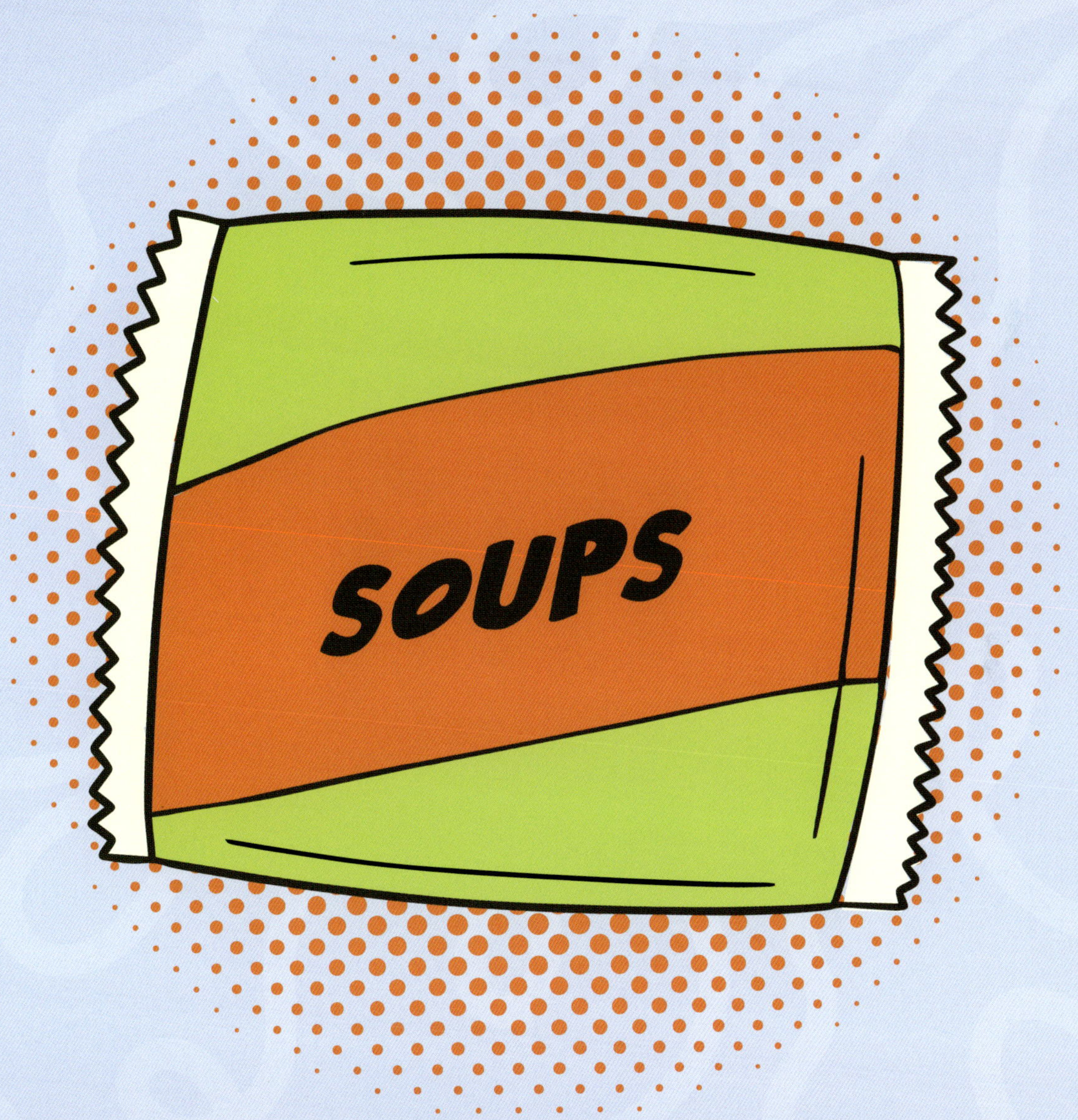
SOUPS

ASIAN CHICKEN NOODLE SOUP

SERVES 2

Scallions, soy sauce, and cilantro give this otherwise traditional chicken soup recipe an Asian edge. It's a nice quick lunch and goes well with a toasted cheese sandwich.

INGREDIENTS

- 2 teaspoons extra-virgin olive oil
- 1 carrot, peeled, halved lengthwise, and thinly sliced into half-moons
- 1 rib celery, thinly sliced
- 2 scallions, white and light green parts, thinly sliced
- 1 boneless, skinless chicken thigh, cut into bite-size pieces
- 2 cups water
- 1 (3-ounce) package ramen noodles, chicken flavor
- ½ teaspoon soy sauce
- 1 tablespoon chopped fresh cilantro

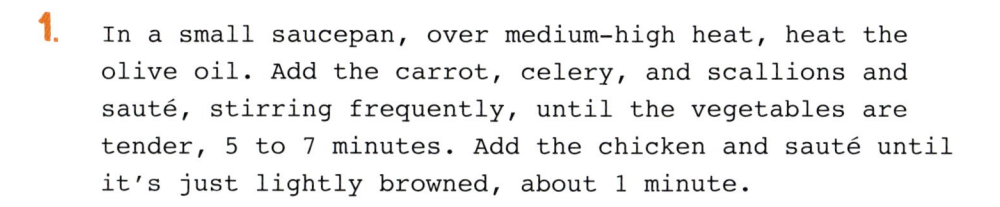

1. In a small saucepan, over medium-high heat, heat the olive oil. Add the carrot, celery, and scallions and sauté, stirring frequently, until the vegetables are tender, 5 to 7 minutes. Add the chicken and sauté until it's just lightly browned, about 1 minute.

2. Add the water and the ramen seasoning. Bring to a simmer over medium-high heat, then lower the heat to medium-low and simmer until the chicken is cooked through, 5 to 7 minutes. Add the ramen noodles and cook until the noodles are tender, about 3 minutes. Stir in the soy sauce.

3. Serve in bowls, garnished with the cilantro.

VIETNAMESE NOODLE SOUP

SERVES 2

One of my favorite soups of all time is pho, a fragrant broth with chewy noodles and plenty of fresh toppings like crisp mung beans, pungent herbs, and tangy lime wedges. Most Vietnamese cooks and restaurants jealously guard their recipe for pho's unctuous, complexly flavored broth, but I've done my best to replicate the spicy, meaty, rich flavor.

INGREDIENTS

- 4 ounces flank steak or hanger steak
- 4 cups beef broth
- ½ onion, thinly sliced
- 1 cinnamon stick
- 1 (2-inch) piece fresh lemongrass, halved lengthwise
- 1 (1-inch) piece fresh ginger, peeled and sliced
- 2 star anise pods
- ½ teaspoon ground coriander
- 2 teaspoons fish sauce
- 1 tablespoon brown sugar (optional)
- 1 (3-ounce) package ramen noodles, any flavor

GARNISHES
- Fresh mung beans
- Lime wedges
- Hoisin sauce
- Sriracha sauce
- Fresh basil leaves
- Fresh mint leaves

1. Trim the steak of excess fat. Slice across the grain as thinly as possible; to get thinner slices, place the beef in the freezer for 20 to 30 minutes to firm it before cutting.

2. In a medium saucepan, combine the beef broth, onion, cinnamon, lemongrass, ginger, star anise, coriander, and fish sauce. Bring to a boil over medium-high heat, then turn down the heat to low and simmer for 30 minutes. Strain out and discard the solids, then return the broth to the saucepan and taste it, adding the brown sugar, if desired. Add the ramen noodles to the broth and simmer for 3 minutes (discard the ramen seasoning).

3. To serve, arrange the garnishes on a platter. Divide the beef between two soup bowls, draping it in the bottom. Bring the broth and noodles to a boil, then immediately divide it between the bowls, pouring it over the beef. The hot broth will cook the beef. Spoon the soup into the bowls. Serve with the platter of garnishes.

THAI COCONUT-LEMONGRASS SOUP

SERVES 2

When I'm under the weather, the Thai soup called *tom kha kai* is as restorative as chicken noodle soup. The ramen noodles help soak up the deliciously rich broth and make this into a substantial one-pot meal. You can use light coconut milk in this recipe, but it won't be as rich or as thick.

INGREDIENTS

1 (13½-ounce) can coconut milk
1 (2-inch) piece fresh lemongrass
1 teaspoon grated fresh ginger
1 teaspoon Thai chili sauce
2 tablespoons fish sauce
1 tablespoon brown sugar
1 boneless, skinless chicken breast, trimmed of excess fat, cut into bite-size pieces
1 (3-ounce) package ramen noodles, any flavor
Juice of 1 lime
1 tablespoon chopped cilantro

1. In a small saucepan over medium-high heat, combine the coconut milk, lemongrass, ginger, chili sauce, fish sauce, and brown sugar. Bring to a simmer, then add the chicken and simmer, stirring occasionally, until the chicken is cooked through, about 5 minutes.

2. Add the ramen noodles and simmer for 3 minutes longer (discard the ramen seasoning). Stir in the lime juice to taste.

3. Serve in bowls garnished with the cilantro.

> **VARIATION**
>
> Use 2 boneless, skinless chicken thighs instead of the breast meat. Thigh meat is a little richer and more flavorful.

TOMATO SOUP WITH PARMESAN RAMEN CROUTONS

SERVES 2

A good bowl of tomato soup is indeed one of life's greatest pleasures. There are some great canned varieties on the market, but every so often I like to make my own. It's not difficult, and the flavor is fresher and more complex than what you can get from canned. Float a Parmesan Ramen Crouton on top for a nice texture contrast and visual appeal. This soup is great alongside a BLT or a grilled cheese sandwich.

INGREDIENTS

2 Parmesan Ramen Croutons (page 149)
1 tablespoon unsalted butter
½ medium onion, chopped
1 carrot, peeled and chopped
1 rib celery, chopped

1 clove garlic, chopped
1 (14-ounce) can crushed tomatoes
2 cups water
1 bay leaf
¼ cup heavy cream
Salt and pepper

1. First, make the croutons (reserve the ramen seasoning).

2. In a medium saucepan over medium heat, melt the butter. Add the onion, carrot, and celery and sauté, stirring occasionally, until the vegetables are tender, about 10 minutes. Add the garlic and sauté, stirring constantly, about 30 seconds.

3. Add the tomatoes, reserved ramen seasoning, water, and bay leaf. Bring to a simmer, then lower the heat and simmer until the vegetables are very tender, 20 to 25 minutes. Remove the bay leaf.

4. Allow the soup to cool slightly, then puree in a blender or a food processor, or use an immersion blender directly in the pan.

5. Return the soup to the pan, stir in the cream, and season to taste with salt and pepper.

6. To serve, ladle soup into two bowls and float a Parmesan Ramen Crouton on top of each one.

SPICY BEEF AND MUSHROOM STEW

SERVES 2

This hearty, beefy stew has an addictively spicy edge thanks to the ramen seasoning packet. The recipe calls for wine to deglaze the pan; the liquid loosens all the flavorful browned bits from the pan so they can mix into the sauce or broth. If you would prefer not to use alcohol, you can use a tablespoon of balsamic vinegar mixed with a tablespoon of beef broth.

INGREDIENTS

- 2 teaspoons extra-virgin olive oil
- ½ onion, cut in half and sliced
- 1 rib celery, thinly sliced
- 1 carrot, peeled, halved lengthwise, and thinly sliced
- 1 cup quartered cremini or white mushrooms
- 6 ounces flank steak or hanger steak, cut into bite-size pieces
- 2 tablespoons red wine
- 1 cup beef stock or broth
- 1 cup water
- 1 (3-ounce) package ramen noodles, chili flavor

1. In a medium saucepan over medium-high heat, heat the olive oil. Add the onion, celery, and carrot and sauté, stirring occasionally, until the vegetables are softened, about 5 minutes. Add the mushrooms and steak and sauté, stirring, until the steak is browned and the mushrooms are soft, 2 to 3 minutes. Add the wine and sauté, scraping the browned bits off the bottom of the pan, until most of the liquid has evaporated, 1 to 2 minutes.

2. Add the stock or broth, water, and ramen seasoning. Bring to a simmer, then turn down the heat to low and simmer for 10 minutes.

3. Break the noodles into pieces, submerge them in the stew, and cook until soft, about 3 minutes. Serve immediately.

Cooked or uncooked, ramen noodles are always a useful ingredient to keep on hand for making salads. They can add crunch to slaw or green salads, especially as a sprinkle seasoned with cheese and dried herbs. Cooked and chilled, they make delicious noodle salads that are perfect to pack in a lunch for work or school or to tote to a picnic or a potluck. As I was testing these salads, I shared many of them at neighborhood get-togethers and was pleasantly surprised by how many requests I got for the recipes!

When I was growing up, my mother would often serve noodles of some sort as a side dish: macaroni and cheese, herbed noodles in a creamy sauce, or cold pasta salad. Somehow, they went with everything, whether we were having fried chicken, steak, or broiled fish. A package of ramen noodles in the pantry and a few more ingredients means you can quickly and easily round out a dinner in a variety of ways. Like the noodle dishes that my mom used to rely on, the assortment of recipes in this chapter should be enough to accompany your main courses, whatever might be in the oven or on the stove.

SALADS AND SIDES

CAESAR SALAD WITH PARMESAN RAMEN CROUTONS

SERVES 4

My college friend HeeJai helped broaden my culinary horizons after I graduated from a Midwestern state school. When I followed her to live in Chicago, she introduced me to Thai noodles, sushi, and Indian food, and she and her sisters taught me lessons about cooking and entertaining that still influence me today. The dressing for this Caesar salad is adapted from one she often made for dinner parties. It's a bit garlicky, but I love the fresh, bright flavor and the easy, no-mess way that it's made in a zip-top bag.

INGREDIENTS

- 1 clove garlic, minced
- 2 tablespoons extra-virgin olive oil
- 2 tablespoons plain yogurt
- 2 tablespoons mashed anchovies
- 1 dash Worcestershire sauce
- 1 tablespoon fresh lemon juice
- 1 head romaine lettuce, torn into bite-size pieces
- 1 recipe Parmesan Ramen Croutons (page 149)

1. In a 1-gallon zip-top bag, combine the garlic, olive oil, yogurt, anchovies, and Worcestershire sauce. Seal the bag and use your fingers on the outside of the bag to mash the ingredients together.

2. Just before serving, add the lemon juice and mash to combine. Add the lettuce to the bag, seal it, and shake to coat the leaves with dressing.

3. To serve, divide the dressed lettuce among four chilled salad plates. Top with the Parmesan Ramen Croutons.

RAMEN-N-CHEESE

SERVES 4

This version of macaroni and cheese gives the impression of being lighter than the traditional dish by using the ramen noodles in place of macaroni. However, the cheese sauce packs a flavorful punch, incorporating the chicken seasoning to enrich the flavor.

INGREDIENTS

- 2 (3-ounce) packages ramen noodles, chicken flavor
- 2½ tablespoons unsalted butter, divided
- 1 tablespoon all-purpose flour
- ½ teaspoon ground dry mustard
- ½ cup milk, divided
- ½ cup cream
- 1½ cups shredded sharp Cheddar cheese (6 ounces)

1. Set aside half of 1 ramen noodle cake. Break the remaining 1½ noodle cakes into quarters and cook in boiling water for 3 minutes, or according to the package instructions (reserve 1 packet ramen seasoning, discard the other). Drain the noodles, reserving the cooking liquid.

2. Break the reserved ½ noodle cake into the bowl of a food processor and pulse until ground into a fine powder, the consistency of fine bread crumbs.

3. In a small bowl in the microwave or in a small saucepan, melt ½ tablespoon of the butter. Off heat, add the ramen crumbs and stir to coat. If using a small saucepan, transfer the crumbs to a small bowl. Set aside.

4. In a small saucepan over low heat, melt the remaining 2 tablespoons butter. Whisk in the flour and continue whisking for 1 minute. Add the reserved ramen seasoning and the dry mustard and whisk to combine. Add ¼ cup of the milk and whisk continuously to combine. Add the remaining ¼ cup milk and the cream and whisk to combine. Turn the heat up to medium-high and cook, whisking constantly, until the mixture begins to thicken, about 4 minutes. Turn the heat to low and whisk in the cheese, ¼ cup at a time, until combined. If the cheese sauce is too thick, add the reserved noodle cooking liquid 1 tablespoon at a time. Add the cooked ramen and stir to combine.

5. Preheat the oven to 350°F. Coat the inside of a medium baking dish (8 or 9 inches square) with cooking spray.

6. Spoon the ramen and cheese mixture into the dish and sprinkle with the ground ramen crumbs. Bake until the ramen crumbs are browned, about 15 minutes. Serve immediately.

COLD NOODLE SALAD WITH GRILLED BEEF

SERVES 2

This is by far one of my favorite recipes in this book—it's the perfect combination of grilled beef, red onions, and chewy noodles dressed in a tangy seasoning, garnished with fresh cilantro. It makes a fantastic main-course salad for dinner or lunch. This dish is easy to make in a grill pan, but if you have an outdoor grill (or an electric countertop grill), by all means, use it!

INGREDIENTS

8 ounces flank steak, trimmed of excess fat
1 red onion, halved and sliced
2 tablespoons soy sauce
1 (3-ounce) package ramen noodles, beef flavor
2 tablespoons rice vinegar
½ teaspoon Dijon mustard
1 tablespoon canola oil
2 tablespoons ground peanuts
2 tablespoons chopped fresh cilantro leaves

1. Heat a grill or a grill pan over high heat.

2. Put the steak and onion in a bowl and drizzle with the soy sauce, tossing with tongs or a fork to coat. When the grill or the pan is very hot, spray it with cooking spray or brush it with vegetable oil and add the beef and onion. Cook for 2 to 3 minutes, then flip the beef and turn the onion. Cook 3 minutes longer, then transfer the beef and onion to a plate and keep warm by covering loosely with aluminum foil.

3. Cook the ramen noodles in boiling water for 3 minutes, or according to the package directions (reserve the ramen seasoning).

4. While the noodles are cooking, make the dressing. In a large bowl, whisk together the rice vinegar, mustard, and ¼ teaspoon of the ramen seasoning. While whisking, drizzle in the oil.

5. When the noodles are finished cooking, drain in a colander and rinse with cold water until cool. Transfer the noodles to the bowl with the dressing and toss to coat.

6. To serve, slice the beef into thin strips diagonally. Divide the noodles between two plates or shallow bowls. Place the beef and the onions on the noodles and garnish with the peanuts and fresh cilantro.

CHINESE CHICKEN SALAD

SERVES 6 TO 8

Studded with sweet mandarin oranges, this salad has a retro feel, like something that "ladies who lunch" would have enjoyed after a morning of shopping. Serve it on a bed of lettuce or on a croissant or brioche bun. A rotisserie chicken will provide roughly the right amount of meat; just carve it up and remove the skin. You can also poach some chicken; see page 148.

INGREDIENTS

1 (3-ounce) package ramen noodles, any flavor
⅓ cup sliced or slivered almonds
1 tablespoon unsalted butter
1 teaspoon five-spice powder
1 pound cooked chicken meat, chopped
2 ribs celery, diced
2 scallions, chopped
½ cup chopped water chestnuts
¾ cup drained canned mandarin oranges
¼ cup mayonnaise
Salt and pepper

1. Crumble the ramen noodles into a small bowl (discard the ramen seasoning) and add the almonds.

2. In a small nonstick skillet over medium-high heat, melt the butter. Pour the melted butter into the noodle mixture and stir to coat. Sprinkle with the five-spice powder and stir to distribute. Pour the mixture into the pan and sauté over medium heat, stirring frequently, until the noodles and nuts begin to brown, about 5 minutes. Remove from the heat and let cool.

3. In a bowl, combine the chicken, celery, scallions, water chestnuts, and oranges. Stir in the mayonnaise and season to taste with salt and pepper. Just before serving, stir in the cooled ramen and nut mixture.

SOUTHERN-STYLE SLAW

SERVES 8 TO 10

In the Southern city I live in, a version of this cabbage-ramen slaw shows up at many potlucks and picnics. Since it doesn't contain mayonnaise, it will withstand sitting out on a warm day better than potato salad or creamy coleslaw. Just make sure to stir in the dry noodles just before serving, as they will get a little soggy after they've sat in the dressing for a while. Tip: To get the perfect size of crumbles of dried ramen noodles, put them in a sealed zip-top bag. Lay the bag on the countertop and run a rolling pin back and forth over it a few times.

INGREDIENTS

- ⅔ cup cider vinegar
- ¼ cup extra-virgin olive oil
- ¼ cup brown sugar
- 1 tablespoon poppy seeds
- Salt and pepper
- 1 (16-ounce) package cabbage slaw mix with carrots
- 1 cup chopped broccoli
- 3 scallions, chopped
- ¼ cup crushed peanuts
- 1 (3-ounce) package ramen noodles, any flavor

1. In a small bowl, whisk together the vinegar, oil, and brown sugar, stirring until the sugar is dissolved. Stir in the poppy seeds and season to taste with salt and pepper.

2. In a serving bowl, combine the cabbage slaw mix, broccoli, and scallions. Pour the dressing over the coleslaw and toss to combine completely. Crush the ramen noodles (discard the ramen seasoning). Just before serving, add the peanuts and ramen noodles and toss to distribute them evenly.

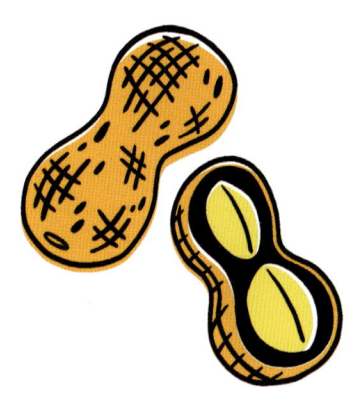

GREEN BEANS WITH CRUNCHY SESAME RAMEN TOPPING

SERVES 2

Dress up plain old green beans with this fun recipe. The inspiration is the classic green bean casserole found on many Thanksgiving tables, but this dish, preferably made with fresh green beans, has a crisper, lighter taste. You can use frozen green beans if you'd like, but try to avoid canned beans, as their flavor and texture is not as good. This dish is excellent alongside a piece of grilled tuna.

INGREDIENTS

1 (3-ounce) package ramen noodles, any flavor
1 tablespoon unsalted butter
2 teaspoons sesame oil, divided
2 teaspoons sugar
1 tablespoon sesame seeds
2 tablespoons canned French fried onions
8 ounces green beans, trimmed
Salt and pepper

1. Crumble the ramen noodles into a small bowl (discard the ramen seasoning).

2. In a medium nonstick skillet over medium heat, melt the butter and add 1 teaspoon of the sesame oil. Add the sugar and stir until the sugar melts and the mixture is a little syrupy. Add the crumbled ramen noodles and the sesame seeds and sauté, stirring frequently, until the noodles are browned and the sesame seeds are clumped together with the ramen bits, 6 to 8 minutes. Remove from the heat, stir in the onions, and set aside.

3. Pour water into a large saucepan to a depth of 1 or 2 inches and put a steamer insert into the pan if you have one. Bring the water to a simmer and add the green beans. Cook until the green beans are bright green and tender, 4 to 6 minutes. Remove from the heat, drain if necessary, and transfer to a serving bowl.

4. Drizzle the beans with the remaining 1 teaspoon sesame oil and a pinch each of salt and pepper. Sprinkle with the ramen-sesame topping and serve hot or warm.

SPAETZLE-STYLE RAMEN NOODLES

SERVES 2 AS A SIDE DISH OR 1 AS A MAIN COURSE

I can't go to a German restaurant without ordering cheese spaetzle, a sautéed noodle dish that usually includes caramelized onions and Emmentaler cheese. Spaetzle is a pain to make at home; you basically drop a soft, batterlike dough into boiling water using a gadget that looks a bit like a cheese grater. But I've found that by using broken ramen noodles, you can at least replicate the taste of this dish, if not the exact texture. Serve this with grilled or sautéed sausages—preferably bratwurst—and a cold beer.

INGREDIENTS

1 teaspoon extra-virgin olive oil
1 medium onion, peeled, halved, and sliced
Salt and pepper
1 (3-ounce) package ramen noodles, any flavor
2 tablespoons unsalted butter
⅓ cup finely shredded Emmentaler cheese (about 1 ounce)
1 tablespoon chopped fresh parsley

1. In a small skillet over medium-low heat, heat the olive oil. Add the onion and cook, stirring occasionally, until brown and caramelized, about 20 minutes. Season with a pinch of salt, remove from the pan, and set aside.

2. While the onions are cooking, break the ramen noodles into about eight pieces and cook in boiling water for 2½ minutes (discard the ramen seasoning). Drain.

3. Wipe out the skillet and place it over medium heat, melt the butter, add the ramen noodles, and sauté until they begin to brown, about 5 minutes. Stir in the onion and the cheese and cook, stirring, until the cheese melts, 3 to 4 minutes. Season to taste with salt and pepper and stir in the parsley.

4. Serve hot.

RAMEN WITH CHERRY TOMATOES AND MOZZARELLA

SERVES 2

This quick pasta dish has a no-cook sauce that's particularly tasty in the summer when tomatoes are at their best. My favorite part about this sauce is how the heat from the pasta melts the mozzarella a little.

INGREDIENTS

1 cup cherry tomatoes, quartered
1 tablespoon chopped kalamata olives
2 tablespoons chopped fresh basil
4 ounces fresh mozzarella, diced
2 tablespoons extra-virgin olive oil
Salt and pepper
1 (3-ounce) package ramen noodles, any flavor
2 tablespoons grated Parmesan cheese

1. In a medium bowl, combine the tomatoes, olives, basil, and mozzarella. Drizzle with the olive oil and stir to combine. Season to taste with the salt and pepper.

2. Cook the ramen noodles in boiling water for 3 minutes, or according to the package directions (discard the ramen seasoning). Drain and return to the pot. Immediately add the tomato mixture and stir to combine. Divide the mixture between two plates or shallow bowls and sprinkle with the Parmesan cheese.

Noodles are as endemic to Asian cuisine as they are to Italian fare—nearly every Asian country and region has at least one type of noodle dish. Take them out of their usual bowl of soup and packaged ramen noodles are a nice element in a variety of Asian noodle dishes, both traditional and modern. What's more, a mound of chewy ramen noodles can be used much in the same way rice is used in Asian cooking: to soak up delicious flavors like Thai curry or the sweet-tart sauce that tops sesame chicken.

Use these recipes as a guide to incorporating ramen noodles into your favorite Asian dishes. And next time you're stir-frying vegetables, boil up a packet of ramen. Ready in just 3 minutes, they take far less time to prepare than a pot of rice!

ASIAN-INSPIRED CLASSICS

PAD THAI

SERVES 2

This traditional Thai noodle dish is usually made with long, chewy rice noodles, but ramen noodles make a fine stand-in. You might be surprised to learn how few ingredients the sauce contains, considering it achieves such a complex-tasting balance of salty, sweet, sour, and spicy. Look for tamarind paste and fish sauce in the Asian section of your supermarket, and refrigerate what you don't use for this dish; both ingredients last for months.

INGREDIENTS

¼ cup brown sugar
3 tablespoons tamarind paste
3 tablespoons fish sauce
2 teaspoons soy sauce
½ teaspoon Thai chili sauce (or to taste)
1 (3-ounce) package ramen noodles, any flavor
2 teaspoons vegetable oil

3 ounces baked tofu, Thai flavor
2 scallions, light green and white parts, thinly sliced
1 large egg

GARNISHES

2 tablespoons chopped peanuts
¼ cup mung beans
1 tablespoon chopped cilantro
2 lime wedges

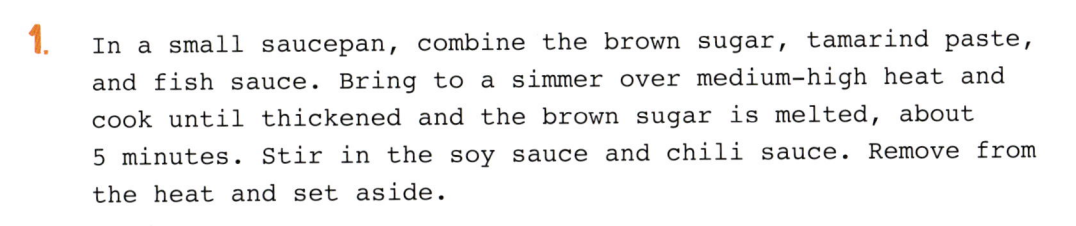

1. In a small saucepan, combine the brown sugar, tamarind paste, and fish sauce. Bring to a simmer over medium-high heat and cook until thickened and the brown sugar is melted, about 5 minutes. Stir in the soy sauce and chili sauce. Remove from the heat and set aside.

2. Break the ramen noodles into four pieces and cook in boiling water for 3 minutes, or according to the package directions (discard the ramen seasoning). Drain.

3. In a medium (10-inch) skillet over high heat, heat the vegetable oil. Add the noodles, tofu, and scallions, and stir-fry for 3 to 5 minutes. Reduce the heat to medium and break the egg into the pan. Stir the egg into the noodle mixture until the egg is scrambled, 45 seconds to 1 minute. Pour the sauce into the pan and cook until all the ingredients are heated through, 2 to 3 minutes, stirring to combine.

4. To serve, transfer to a serving bowl. Garnish with the peanuts, mung beans, cilantro, and lime.

COLD SESAME NOODLES

SERVES 2

At once sweet, spicy, nutty, and cool, sesame noodles have always been one of my favorites on Chinese takeout menus. This is ideal picnic fare: The noodles will stay fresh for a few hours even if they're not refrigerated, and there's nothing in the dish that will spoil.

INGREDIENTS

¼ cup smooth peanut butter
1 tablespoon plus 1 teaspoon rice vinegar
1 teaspoon soy sauce
1 teaspoon brown sugar
½ teaspoon grated fresh ginger
½ teaspoon sesame oil
¼ teaspoon minced garlic
1 (3-ounce) package ramen noodles, any flavor
1 tablespoon sesame seeds, plus more for garnish
1 scallion, green and light green parts, thinly sliced
¼ cup diced peeled cucumber

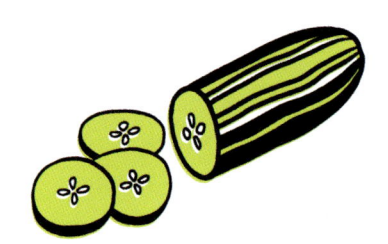

1. In a small bowl, whisk together the peanut butter, rice vinegar, soy sauce, brown sugar, ginger, sesame oil, and garlic. Set aside.

2. Cook the ramen noodles in boiling water for 2½ minutes (discard the ramen seasoning). Drain in a colander then return the hot noodles immediately to the pot. Add the sauce and stir to coat completely. Stir in the sesame seeds.

3. To serve, place the noodles in a bowl and top with the scallions, cucumber, and additional sesame seeds. The noodles will keep, covered and refrigerated, for 2 to 3 days. If the noodles clump together, break them up a little with a fork before serving.

LOADED STIR-FRY

SERVES 2

A good stir-fry recipe means you'll never go hungry, especially if there are miscellaneous vegetables and meats in your refrigerator or freezer. This basic recipe leaves plenty of room for adaptation: Use whatever vegetables you like, or are in season, or happen to be in your crisper; use the kind of meat or seafood you prefer; and adjust the ingredients in the sauce according to the flavors you like best.

INGREDIENTS

- ⅓ cup vegetable or chicken broth
- 2 tablespoons soy sauce
- 1 tablespoon rice cooking wine
- 1 tablespoon brown sugar
- 1 teaspoon sesame oil
- 1 teaspoon cornstarch
- 1 (3-ounce) package ramen noodles, soy sauce flavor
- 1 tablespoon vegetable oil
- 1 clove garlic, minced
- 1 teaspoon minced or grated fresh ginger
- 1 carrot, peeled and thinly sliced
- ½ onion, thinly sliced
- ½ cup packaged cabbage slaw mix
- ½ cup chopped green bell pepper
- ½ cup chopped red bell pepper
- 4 ounces tail-on shrimp, peeled and deveined

1. In a small bowl, whisk together the broth, soy sauce, rice cooking wine, brown sugar, sesame oil, cornstarch, and ramen seasoning. Whisk until the sugar and the cornstarch dissolve.

2. Break the ramen noodles into smaller pieces, if desired, then cook in boiling water for 3 minutes, or according to the package directions. Drain and set aside.

3. In a wok or a large nonstick skillet over high heat, heat the oil. Add the garlic and ginger and cook, stirring constantly, for 30 seconds. Add the carrot, onion, and cabbage slaw mix and stir-fry until the cabbage is slightly wilted and the onion is beginning to turn translucent, 2 to 3 minutes. Add the bell peppers and the shrimp. Stir-fry until the vegetables are crisp-tender and the shrimp are opaque and cooked through, about 5 minutes.

4. Whisk the sauce to recombine the ingredients and pour it over the mixture in the wok. Bring to a boil and simmer until the sauce is thickened and slightly glossy, about 2 minutes, stirring to coat all the ingredients. Stir in the cooked ramen noodles. Serve immediately.

> **VARIATION** Other great additions are edamame, snow peas, shiitakes, broccoli, bok choy, baby corn, water chestnuts, green beans, and scallions. Tofu, chicken, scallops, and beef are good alternatives for the protein.

SESAME-CRUSTED TUNA WITH PONZU GLAZE ON RAMEN NOODLES

SERVES 2

I made a version of this recipe for dinner the night I met my now-husband's parents. It was actually the perfect recipe for such an occasion—it's quick to prepare yet looks and tastes like something you'd get at a nice restaurant. To this day, it's still a recipe I bring out when I need to impress someone.

INGREDIENTS

¼ cup ponzu sauce or soy sauce
2 tablespoons honey
2 teaspoons sesame oil, divided
2 scallions, white and green parts, thinly sliced separately
2 (4-ounce) tuna steaks, about 1 inch thick
½ cup sesame seeds
2 teaspoons vegetable oil
1 (3-ounce) package ramen noodles, any flavor

1. In a zip-top bag or a bowl, combine the ponzu or soy sauce, honey, 1 teaspoon of the sesame oil, and the white part of the scallions. Add the tuna steaks and let marinate for 5 minutes.

2. Place the sesame seeds on a plate or in a shallow bowl. Remove the tuna from the marinade, reserving the marinade, and press the tuna into the sesame seeds, turning to coat all sides.

3. In a small nonstick skillet over high heat, heat the vegetable oil. Add the tuna and cook until the exterior is browned but the interior is still red, 4 to 5 minutes, turning over halfway through cooking. Remove from the pan and keep warm on a plate covered loosely with aluminum foil. Add the marinade to the pan; it should immediately boil and thicken. Remove at once from the heat, stirring rapidly.

4. Cook the ramen noodles in boiling water for 3 minutes or according to the package directions (discard the ramen seasoning). Drain, return to the pot, and toss with the remaining 1 teaspoon sesame oil.

5. Divide the noodles between two plates, thinly slice the tuna, and arrange the slices on the noodles. Drizzle with the glaze and garnish with the green parts of the scallions before serving.

SESAME CHICKEN AND BROCCOLI

SERVES 2

Sesame chicken is a Chinese-restaurant favorite—crisp chicken pieces in a sticky-sweet sauce. The chicken is traditionally fried, but since deep-frying can be messy and involved, I've adapted a version I saw in a magazine in which the chicken is coated in an egg white and cornstarch mixture and pan-fried.

INGREDIENTS

- 3 tablespoons honey
- 2 tablespoons soy sauce
- 1 teaspoon rice vinegar
- 3 tablespoons sesame seeds, divided
- 4 tablespoons vegetable or canola oil, divided
- 3 cups broccoli florets
- 2 scallions, white and green parts, minced separately
- 2 cloves garlic, minced
- 1 large egg white
- 2 tablespoons cornstarch
- 1 pound boneless, skinless chicken breasts or thighs, cut into 1-inch chunks
- Salt and pepper
- 1 (3-ounce) package ramen noodles, any flavor
- 1 teaspoon sesame oil

1. In a small bowl, stir together the honey, soy sauce, rice vinegar, and 2 tablespoons of the sesame seeds. Set aside.

2. In a large nonstick skillet over high heat, heat 1 tablespoon of the oil. Sauté the broccoli and white and light green parts of the scallions until the broccoli is bright green and crisp-tender, about 5 minutes. Add the garlic and cook, stirring constantly, for 30 seconds. Transfer the vegetables to a bowl and cover loosely with aluminum foil to keep warm.

3. Lower the heat to medium-high and add the remaining 3 tablespoons oil to the now-empty pan.

4. In a medium bowl, whisk together the egg white and cornstarch.

5. Season the chicken with salt and pepper and add to the egg white mixture, stirring to coat the chicken completely.

- continued -

6. Using a fork or a slotted spoon, remove the chicken from the bowl, letting any excess egg white drip off, and transfer the chicken to the pan. Cook, turning occasionally, until light golden on all sides and cooked through, 5 to 8 minutes. Cut into a piece if necessary to check doneness; the chicken should not be pink, and its internal temperature should measure 165°F on a meat thermometer.

7. Use a spoon to remove any excess oil from the pan, then add the vegetables back into the pan. Pour the sauce into the pan and stir to combine.

8. Meanwhile, cook the ramen noodles in boiling water for 3 minutes, or according to the package directions (discard the ramen seasoning). Drain and return to the pot.

9. Drizzle with sesame oil and sprinkle with the remaining 1 tablespoon sesame seeds.

10. To serve, divide the noodles between two plates or shallow bowls. Top with the chicken-broccoli mixture and garnish with the reserved dark green parts of the scallions.

89

GREEN COCONUT CURRY SHRIMP BOWL

SERVES 2

Coconut curry sauce can be so addictive, you'll find yourself slurping up every drop, but a tangle of ramen noodles is the best way to soak it up. You can use red curry paste instead of green for a different flavor; many people think one curry is spicier than the other, but that's not really the case. According to Simply Asia Foods (now owned by McCormick & Company), which manufactures the Thai Kitchen product line, red curry paste has a more roasted flavor, while green curry paste typically has more cumin and an earthier taste.

INGREDIENTS

- 2 teaspoons canola or vegetable oil
- 1 small onion, cut in half and sliced
- 1 small red or yellow bell pepper, sliced
- 1 (14-ounce) can coconut milk
- ½ to 2 tablespoons green or red curry paste
- 1 teaspoon brown sugar
- ½ lime
- 6 ounces cooked shrimp, peeled and deveined
- ½ cup frozen peas
- 1 (3-ounce) package ramen noodles, any flavor
- 1 tablespoon chopped fresh cilantro

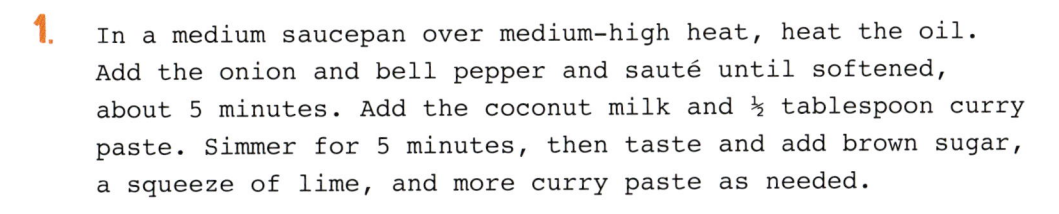

1. In a medium saucepan over medium-high heat, heat the oil. Add the onion and bell pepper and sauté until softened, about 5 minutes. Add the coconut milk and ½ tablespoon curry paste. Simmer for 5 minutes, then taste and add brown sugar, a squeeze of lime, and more curry paste as needed.

2. Add the shrimp and the frozen peas and simmer for 10 minutes, until the shrimp and peas are heated through and the sauce is thickened.

3. Meanwhile, cook the ramen noodles in boiling water for 3 minutes, or according to the package directions (discard the ramen seasoning). Drain.

4. To serve, divide the noodles between two shallow bowls. Ladle the curry mixture over the noodles and garnish with the chopped cilantro.

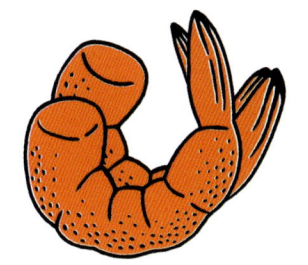

DAN DAN NOODLES

SERVES 2

No two versions of this Sichuan noodle dish seem to be the same in terms of what ingredients they contain or how they're seasoned, but the one element that most share is Sichuan peppercorns. This spice, the dried berry husk from a type of ash tree, has an inimitable tingly spiciness. It was banned for nearly forty years by the U.S. government because of concern that it could spread a disease to American trees. The ban was lifted in 2005, and now it's not hard to find in Asian grocery stores or even in the Asian foods section of many well-stocked supermarkets.

INGREDIENTS

- 1 tablespoon Sichuan peppercorns, ground in a spice grinder or with a mortar and pestle
- 1 tablespoon smooth peanut butter
- 2 tablespoons plus 2 teaspoons soy sauce, divided
- 2 teaspoons chili oil
- 1 teaspoon brown sugar
- 2 teaspoons canola or vegetable oil
- 3 scallions, light green and white parts, thinly sliced separately
- 8 ounces ground pork
- 1 tablespoon grated fresh ginger
- 1 clove garlic, minced
- 1 teaspoon rice cooking wine or dry sherry
- 1 (3-ounce) package ramen noodles, any flavor
- ¼ cup sliced peeled cucumber, cut into matchsticks

1. In a small bowl, stir together the peppercorns, peanut butter, 2 tablespoons of the soy sauce, the chili oil, and brown sugar. Set aside.

2. In a large nonstick skillet over medium-high heat, heat the oil. Set aside 1 tablespoon of the light green scallions, then add the remaining scallions, the pork, ginger, and garlic to the pan and cook, breaking the pork into small crumbles, until the meat is well-cooked, browned, and slightly crispy. Add the rice cooking wine and the remaining 2 teaspoons soy sauce and cook, stirring frequently, until the mixture is nearly dry. Set aside.

3. Cook the ramen noodles in boiling water for 3 minutes, or according to the package directions (discard the ramen seasoning).

4. Drain, transfer to a serving bowl, and toss with the reserved peppercorn sauce. Sprinkle with the cooked pork mixture and serve garnished with the reserved light green scallions and the cucumbers.

STIR-FRIED VEGETABLES IN COCONUT-GINGER SAUCE

SERVES 2

Ramen noodles soak up the delicate, subtly sweet coconut sauce in this surprisingly simple recipe. Use a package of frozen stir-fry vegetables or any combination of your favorite fresh or frozen veggies.

INGREDIENTS

1 tablespoon vegetable or canola oil
2 cups frozen stir-fry vegetables
1 clove garlic, minced
1 teaspoon minced ginger
¾ cup coconut milk
Juice of 1 lime
1 teaspoon soy sauce
Pinch of red pepper flakes
1 (3-ounce) package ramen noodles, any flavor

1. In a large nonstick skillet over medium- heat, heat the oil. When the oil is hot, add the vegetables and cook, stirring frequently, until the vegetables are crisp-tender, 5 to 7 minutes. Add the garlic and ginger and cook, stirring constantly, for 30 seconds. Add the coconut milk and simmer over medium-high heat, stirring occasionally, until the sauce is slightly thickened, 5 to 7 minutes. Season to taste with the lime juice, soy sauce, and red pepper flakes.

2. While the vegetables are cooking, cook the ramen noodles in boiling water for 3 minutes, or according to the package directions (discard the ramen seasoning). Drain.

3. Serve the vegetable mixture over the cooked ramen noodles or stir the noodles into the vegetable mixture in the pan.

Ramen can stand in for other types of noodles in a wide range of recipes. The nice thing is that they cook in a fraction of the time of most other noodles, so it really speeds up the cooking process. Using the dry noodles ground up in place of bread crumbs makes them even more versatile, as in meat loaf and crusted chicken or fish recipes.

Home-Style Comfort Foods

RAMEN ALFREDO WITH ASPARAGUS

SERVES 2

Decadent Alfredo sauce is a wonderful indulgence. I love the way the sauce clings to skinny ramen noodles, and a handful of asparagus can cut the richness a little.

INGREDIENTS

1 cup heavy cream
4 tablespoons unsalted butter, cut into pieces
½ cup Parmesan cheese, plus more for serving
½ teaspoon garlic powder
Pinch of nutmeg
Black pepper
1 (3-ounce) package ramen noodles, any flavor
1 cup chopped fresh or frozen asparagus (1-inch pieces)

1. In a medium saucepan over medium heat, heat the cream to a simmer. Add the butter and stir occasionally until completely melted. Add the cheese, garlic powder, and nutmeg. Simmer over medium-low heat, stirring frequently, until the cheese is melted and the mixture is smooth and creamy, about 5 minutes. Season to taste with pepper.

2. Meanwhile, cook the ramen noodles and asparagus for 3 minutes in boiling water (discard the ramen seasoning). Drain and return to the pot. Stir in the sauce to coat the noodles completely.

3. To serve, divide the noodles between two bowls and sprinkle with additional Parmesan cheese.

> **VARIATION**
>
> Omit the asparagus. Mix the noodles with the sauce and top each serving with ½ cup sautéed wild mushrooms.

INDIVIDUAL TURKEY MEAT LOAVES WITH CRUNCHY RAMEN TOPPING

SERVES 4

Everyone knows that the best part of meat loaf is the slightly crunchy, sticky-sweet ends. If you make individual meat loaves, nobody has to fight over who gets the two coveted end pieces. Plus, mini loaves will cook faster than one large loaf. If you don't have a food processor to grind the ramen noodles, you can put the dry noodles in a zip-top bag, lay the bag on a countertop or a table, and crush the noodles with a pan or rolling pin. The cooked meat loaves keep well in the refrigerator for 2 to 3 days, or in the freezer, wrapped tightly in plastic wrap, for up to 6 months.

INGREDIENTS

- 1 (3-ounce) package ramen noodles, any flavor
- ½ medium onion, finely chopped
- 1 pound ground turkey
- ¼ cup ketchup
- 3 tablespoons teriyaki sauce, divided
- 1 teaspoon dried thyme
- 1 large egg

1. Preheat the oven to 350°F. Line a 9 x 13-inch baking pan with aluminum foil and spray the foil with cooking spray.

2. Break the ramen noodles into the bowl of a food processor and pulse to grind until they resemble rolled oats (discard the ramen seasoning). Set aside 2 tablespoons of the ground ramen.

3. In a large bowl, stir together the onion, turkey, the remaining ground ramen, the ketchup, 1 tablespoon of the teriyaki sauce, and the thyme.

4. In a small bowl, whisk the egg lightly, then stir it into the turkey mixture. You can use your hands to make sure the mixture is thoroughly combined.

5. Form the turkey mixture into four loaves and put them on the prepared baking pan. Brush the loaves with the remaining 2 tablespoons teriyaki sauce and sprinkle them with the remaining 2 tablespoons ground ramen noodles.

6. Bake until the meat loaves are cooked through and the tops are browned, 30 to 40 minutes. The internal temperature of the meat loaves should be 165°F on a meat thermometer.

RAMEN-CRUSTED CHICKEN FINGERS WITH HONEY MUSTARD SAUCE

SERVES 4

Dry ramen noodles make a crunchy, flavorful topping for chicken pieces. Kids will like eating these as finger foods, dipped into the honey mustard, ketchup, or sweet and tangy barbecue sauce. You can also serve them as a chicken satay—style appetizer, on skewers and with peanut sauce for dipping, or you can use them to top a green salad.

INGREDIENTS

- 1 (3-ounce) package ramen noodles, chicken flavor
- ⅛ cup yellow mustard
- ⅛ cup honey
- 1 pound boneless, skinless chicken breast or chicken cutlets, cut into strips

1. Preheat the oven to 400°F and line a rimmed baking sheet with parchment paper.

2. Break the ramen noodles into the bowl of a food processor and pulse until the noodles are ground into small pieces, about the consistency of rolled oats. Transfer to a shallow bowl and mix with the ramen seasoning.

3. In a small bowl, stir together the mustard and honey. Spoon 1 to 2 tablespoons honey mustard into a second shallow bowl and reserve the rest for a dipping sauce.

4. Pat the chicken pieces dry with a paper towel and brush them with the honey mustard, then roll each piece in the ramen mixture, making sure to coat the chicken completely.

5. Transfer the chicken pieces to the prepared baking sheet. Spray the chicken lightly with cooking spray and bake for 10 minutes. Turn the chicken pieces over, spray lightly with the cooking spray again, and bake until the chicken is cooked through, 5 to 10 minutes longer. If you cut into a piece of chicken, it should not be pink, and its internal temperature should measure 165°F on a meat thermometer.

6. Serve with the remaining honey mustard sauce or barbecue sauce.

RAMEN BOLOGNESE

SERVES 2

Sometimes a little red-sauce pasta is just what you need, and a package of ramen noodles is the perfect amount for two (or for one healthy appetite). Set out a red-checkered tablecloth and a bottle of Chianti and toast some garlic bread for a delicious Italian-style supper, just like Nonna used to make. Just don't tell her you used ramen noodles in place of Italian spaghetti!

INGREDIENTS

1 tablespoon extra-virgin olive oil
1 small onion, diced
1 clove garlic, minced
4 ounces ground turkey or ground beef
1 (15-ounce) can crushed tomatoes
1 tablespoon tomato paste
1 tablespoon dried Italian herbs
Salt and pepper
1 (3-ounce) package ramen noodles, any flavor
Grated Parmesan cheese, for serving

1. In a medium saucepan over medium-high heat, heat the olive oil. Add the onion and sauté, stirring occasionally, until translucent and softened, about 5 minutes. Add the garlic and cook, stirring constantly, for 30 seconds. Add the beef or turkey and cook, breaking up the large chunks, until the meat is browned and cooked through, 5 to 7 minutes. Tilt the pan and use a spoon to remove excess oil or cooking liquid.

2. Stir in the tomatoes, tomato paste, and Italian herbs. Bring to a boil, then lower the heat and simmer for 10 minutes to allow the flavors to meld. Season to taste with salt and pepper.

3. While the sauce is simmering, cook the ramen noodles in boiling water for 3 minutes, or according to the package directions (discard the ramen seasoning). Drain the noodles.

4. To serve, divide the noodles between two bowls and top with Bolognese sauce. Sprinkle with Parmesan cheese.

BEEF STROGANOFF ON BUTTERED PARSLEY RAMEN NOODLES

SERVES 2

This hearty recipe has a rich, creamy, satisfying flavor. The fresh parsley gives this dish a fresh, bright contrast to the creaminess of the sauce and adds a bit of color.

INGREDIENTS

- 1 tablespoon plus 1 teaspoon unsalted butter, divided
- 1 shallot or ½ small onion, minced
- ½ cup sliced cremini mushrooms (5 ounces)
- 8 ounces flank steak or hanger steak, cut into thin strips
- Salt and pepper
- ¼ cup low-fat sour cream
- 1 (3-ounce) package ramen noodles, any flavor
- 1 tablespoon chopped fresh parsley, plus more for garnish

1. In a medium nonstick skillet over medium heat, melt 1 tablespoon of the butter. When the butter begins to foam, add the shallot or onion and cook until softened and translucent, 2 to 3 minutes. Add the mushrooms and cook until softened, stirring occasionally, 3 to 4 minutes. Season the steak with salt and pepper and add it to the pan. Cook on medium-high heat until cooked through, stirring and turning over the pieces, 3 to 4 minutes. Lower the heat to medium-low and stir in the sour cream. Season to taste with salt and pepper.

2. While you're cooking the steak, cook the ramen noodles in boiling water for 3 minutes, or according to the package directions (discard the ramen seasoning). Drain, return to the pot, and add the remaining 1 teaspoon butter and the parsley.

3. To serve, divide the noodles between two plates or shallow bowls and top with the steak and mushroom mixture. Garnish with more parsley.

KALE-CHEDDAR NOODLE CASSEROLE

SERVES 4

This riff on macaroni and cheese includes kale, a hearty green that's super-nutritious and has a nice bite to it. You can also use spinach, mustard greens, or any other leafy green. Kale often is available chopped and prewashed in a bag, which makes putting together this baked dish even easier.

INGREDIENTS

2½ cups chopped kale (about 1 bunch)

2½ (3-ounce) packages ramen noodles, any flavor, divided

2 tablespoons unsalted butter, divided

¼ teaspoon garlic powder, plus more for topping, divided

2 tablespoons grated Parmesan cheese

1 tablespoon all-purpose flour

1 cup milk

½ teaspoon Dijon mustard

1 cup shredded Cheddar cheese (4 ounces)

½ teaspoon salt

1. Preheat the oven to 350°F. Butter the bottom and sides of a small baking dish (about 8 inches square).

2. Bring a medium pot of water to a boil over high heat. Add the kale and boil for 3 minutes. Add 2 packages of the ramen noodles and boil for 3 minutes longer (discard the ramen seasoning). Drain the noodles and kale, return to the pot, and cover with a lid to keep warm.

3. To make the crunchy ramen topping, break the remaining ½ package ramen noodles into the bowl of a food processor and pulse to grind until they resemble rolled oats (discard the ramen seasoning). Transfer the ground noodles to a small bowl. Melt 1 tablespoon of the butter in the microwave and add it to the dry noodles, as well as a pinch of garlic powder and the Parmesan cheese. Stir to combine and set aside.

4. In a medium saucepan, melt the remaining 1 tablespoon butter. Whisk in the flour and cook for 1 minute, until the mixture forms a clumpy paste. Gradually whisk in the milk, whisking after each addition until the mixture is smooth, to avoid lumps. When all the milk is incorporated, simmer, whisking frequently, until the mixture is thick and creamy, about 7 minutes. Stir in the mustard, cheese, salt, and remaining ¼ teaspoon garlic powder and cook over low heat until the cheese is completely melted, 4 to 5 minutes. Pour the cheese mixture over the noodles and kale and stir to combine.

5. Transfer the noodle-cheese mixture to the prepared baking dish. Sprinkle the topping evenly over the noodles and bake uncovered until heated through and bubbling, 15 to 20 minutes.

ZUCCHINI BOATS FILLED WITH RAMEN AND MUSHROOMS

SERVES 4 AS A MAIN COURSE OR 8 AS A SIDE DISH

Roasted zucchini stuffed with a tasty filling never fails to impress. In this recipe, the filling is a mixture of sautéed mushrooms, meatless crumbles, and ramen noodles, all smothered with gooey melted mozzarella cheese. Kids especially love these "boats" and how the zucchini makes a bowl of sorts for the hearty filling.

INGREDIENTS

- 4 small zucchini
- 1 (3-ounce) package ramen noodles, any flavor
- 2 teaspoons extra-virgin olive oil
- ½ cup diced onion
- 4 ounces cremini mushrooms, sliced
- ½ teaspoon dried Italian herbs or dried oregano
- ½ teaspoon ground cumin
- Salt and pepper
- ½ cup frozen meatless crumbles, like MorningStar Farms
- ¾ cup canned chopped tomatoes
- 1 cup shredded mozzarella cheese (4 ounces)

1. Preheat the oven to 375°F. Line a rimmed baking sheet with parchment paper.

2. Cut the stems off the zucchini and cut them in half lengthwise. Hollow out each half by scooping out the seeds and some of the flesh. Put the zucchini cut-side down on the prepared baking sheet and bake until slightly softened, about 15 minutes. Remove from the oven and turn the zucchini over so the hollow side is facing up. Preheat the broiler.

3. While the zucchini bakes, cook the ramen noodles in boiling water for 3 minutes, or according to the package directions (discard the ramen seasoning). Drain and set aside.

4. In a large nonstick skillet over medium-high heat, heat the olive oil. Add the onion and sauté until translucent, 3 to 4 minutes. Add the mushrooms and cook until soft, 7 to 9 minutes. Add the herbs and the cumin and season to taste with salt and pepper.

5. Add the meatless crumbles and cook until heated through. Stir in the noodles and tomatoes and cook, stirring occasionally, until the mixture is heated through, 4 to 5 minutes.

6. Divide the filling between the zucchini boats. Sprinkle evenly with cheese and broil until the cheese melts, about 3 minutes. Serve immediately.

When you're cooking for guests, it doesn't seem like ramen would be the type of meal that would impress them. But think again—with upscale ingredients and special techniques, even ramen can be part of a stellar meal. Challenge your culinary skills with these recipes that are sure to be a hit at your dinner table.

Cooking for Company or a Crowd

PARTY ON!

Make your mealtime more special, whether you're cooking for a significant other, hosting a dinner party, or just celebrating the end of the week. Here's how:

- A tablecloth or place mats, and cloth napkins, can really dress up the table and add to a restaurant-quality experience. If you have good china, now's the time to get it out.

- For a dinner party, serve an appetizer, even if it's something simple like dishes of nuts or olives, or a cheese plate. You can set out the appetizers in the living room so that your guests can relax and mingle while you're in the kitchen, putting last-minute touches on the meal.

- Make a playlist or mix of your favorite music to play in the background. Well-chosen music puts everyone in a more relaxed mood and really adds to a festive atmosphere.

- As you're cooking, clean as you go, and try to wash and put away dishes and wipe down counters just before your guests arrive. Most dinner parties eventually end up in the kitchen, so you'll want it looking decent. Plus, an empty sink and clean counters will make it easier to clear the table and clean up after your meal.

- Don't forget the beverages! Search online for a fun, easy cocktail or sangria to make, choose a few bottles of wine, or make a batch of fresh lemonade or iced tea. Having a few choices on hand—with and without alcohol—will ensure that you can please everybody. Put a pitcher of ice water on the table, too.

- Next time you're agonizing over what appealing dish to serve at a party or tote to a potluck, just pull a couple of packages of ramen noodles out of your pantry. You can't miss: Ramen is inexpensive, it cooks quickly, and it appeals to kids and adults alike. Plus, it's endlessly versatile—from a coconut-spiked fruit salad to a baked casserole, you'll be set for your next shindig.

SOY GRILLED TOFU ON GINGERY NOODLES

SERVES 2

You don't have to serve meat for an elegant dinner. Tofu, when it's cut into "steaks," marinated, and grilled, makes a fine main course.

INGREDIENTS

2 tablespoons soy sauce
1 teaspoon sesame oil
1 (14-ounce) block extra-firm tofu, sliced in half lengthwise
1 (3-ounce) package ramen noodles, any flavor
¼ cup seasoned rice vinegar
¼ teaspoon grated fresh ginger
2 tablespoons chopped cashews
1 tablespoon chopped fresh mint

1. Heat a grill pan, electric grill, or gas or charcoal grill on high heat.

2. In a small bowl, stir together the soy sauce and sesame oil. Brush both sides of the tofu with the soy sauce mixture.

3. Grill the tofu until grill marks appear, about 5 minutes. Flip and grill for 5 minutes longer on the second side.

4. Meanwhile, cook the ramen noodles in boiling water for 3 minutes, or according to the package directions (discard the ramen seasoning).

5. In a small bowl, combine the rice vinegar and ginger. Drain the noodles, return to the pot, and drizzle with the vinegar mixture. Toss to coat.

6. To serve, divide the noodles between two shallow bowls or plates. Place a tofu steak on each bed of noodles. Garnish with the cashews and mint.

TEMPURA SHRIMP IN MISO-SCALLION SOUP

SERVES 4

Deep-frying is a bit of a production, but it's worth the effort for guests. Just be sure you're ready to serve the shrimp right when they come out of the hot oil—tempura is best when it's hot.

INGREDIENTS

- 1 tablespoon wakame (dried seaweed)
- 4 cups plus 4 tablespoons water, divided
- 2 scallions, thinly sliced
- 1 pound soft tofu, cut into small cubes
- 3 tablespoons white miso
- 2 (3-ounce) packages ramen noodles, any flavor
- Dash of soy sauce
- Vegetable or canola oil, for deep-frying
- 1½ cups all-purpose flour, divided
- ½ cup rice flour
- 1 large egg
- ¾ cup cold seltzer water
- 8 uncooked tail-on shrimp, peeled and deveined, patted dry

1. In a small bowl, soak the wakame in 2 tablespoons of the water for 10 minutes.

2. In a large saucepan, combine 4 cups of the water, the soaked wakame, the scallions, and tofu. Bring to a simmer over medium-high heat and cook for 5 minutes.

3. While the broth simmers, in a small bowl, combine the miso with just enough water to make a thin paste, about 2 tablespoons, stirring until smooth. Remove the broth from the heat and stir in the miso. Set aside.

4. Cook the ramen noodles in boiling water for 3 minutes, or according to the package directions (discard the ramen seasoning). Drain and set aside.

5. Pour oil into a large, heavy-bottomed pot to a depth of 3 inches. Heat the oil over medium-high heat until the temperature is 350° to 375°F on a deep-frying thermometer, about 10 minutes. When the oil is ready, lower the heat to maintain the proper temperature.

6. While the oil is heating, in a bowl, combine ½ cup of the all-purpose flour and the rice flour. Using a fork, stir in the egg and gradually stir in the cold seltzer water until the mixture is about the consistency of thick pancake batter. Place the remaining 1 cup flour in a medium bowl. Line a rimmed baking sheet with paper towels and set it next to the stove.

– continued –

7. When the oil is ready, dredge a shrimp in the flour, dusting off any excess, then, holding the shrimp by its tail, dip it into the batter, holding it for a moment over the bowl to let any excess batter drip off. Carefully drop the battered shrimp into the hot oil and repeat with the remaining shrimp, adding only as many at one time as will fit in the pot without crowding. Fry for 3 minutes, turning the shrimp over with a slotted spoon halfway through cooking. Transfer the cooked shrimp to the prepared baking sheet. Repeat the battering and cooking process with the remaining shrimp if necessary.

8. To serve, stir the noodles into the miso broth. Ladle the soup into four bowls, then rest two tempura shrimp in each bowl, leaning the tail against the edge of the bowl.

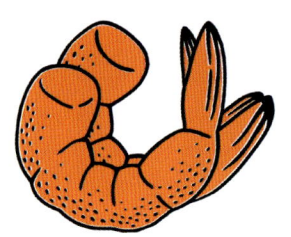

TUNA NOODLE CASSEROLE

SERVES 8 TO 10

This casserole is a riff on the traditional casseroles that call for a can of condensed cream of mushroom soup. Instead, fresh mushrooms and a roux (a mixture of melted butter and flour that is used to thicken a mixture) makes the creamy sauce. It's great on a cold winter night with a green salad and a loaf of bread.

INGREDIENTS

- 5 tablespoons unsalted butter, divided
- 1 large onion, chopped (about 1 cup)
- 8 ounces sliced cremini or white mushrooms
- 4 (3-ounce) packages ramen noodles, chicken flavor, divided
- 1 tablespoon red wine vinegar
- 2 teaspoons soy sauce
- ¼ cup all-purpose flour
- 1 cup chicken broth
- 1¼ cups milk
- 1½ cups frozen peas
- 1 (12-ounce) can chunk light tuna packed in water, drained
- 1 tablespoon dried thyme
- Salt and pepper
- ¼ teaspoon hot sauce (or to taste)
- 1 cup shredded Colby or Cheddar cheese (4 ounces)

- continued -

1. Preheat the oven to 375°F. Spray a 9 x 13-inch glass baking dish with cooking spray or rub with butter. Bring a large pot of water to a boil over high heat.

2. In a large nonstick skillet over medium-high heat, melt 1 tablespoon of the butter. Add the onion and cook until softened, about 5 minutes. Add the mushrooms and cook until they release their liquid and the liquid evaporates, 5 to 7 minutes. Stir in 1 teaspoon of the ramen seasoning (discard the remainder), the red wine vinegar, and soy sauce and cook until most of the liquid has reduced, 1 to 2 minutes longer. Set aside.

3. In a medium saucepan over medium heat, melt 3 tablespoons of the butter. When the butter foams, whisk in the flour and continue whisking until the flour and butter form a thick paste, 1 to 2 minutes. Slowly whisk in the chicken broth and then the milk, whisking between additions until the mixture is smooth and lump-free. When all the liquid has been added, bring to a simmer and cook until thickened, about 5 minutes, whisking frequently to make sure that the mixture doesn't stick to the bottom and scorch. With a wooden spoon, stir in the mushroom mixture, peas, tuna, and thyme.

4. Break 3 packages of the ramen noodles into four pieces each and cook them in boiling water for 2½ minutes. Drain and return to the pot. Add the tuna mixture and stir to combine completely. Season to taste with salt and pepper. Season with the hot sauce. Transfer the casserole mixture to the prepared baking dish.

5. Break the remaining 1 package ramen noodles into the bowl of a food processor and pulse until it resembles fine bread crumbs. Transfer to a bowl.

6. Melt the remaining 1 tablespoon butter in the microwave and drizzle over the noodles. Stir in the cheese. Sprinkle the ground ramen over the casserole.

7. Bake until the cheese is melted, 20 to 30 minutes. Serve hot.

SALMON CROQUETTES WITH CREAMY CHILI SAUCE

SERVES 4

Ground in the food processor, dry ramen makes a good stand-in for bread crumbs, and it retains a nice crunch wherever it's used. The chili flavor seasoning packet is used both in the croquette breading and to flavor the yogurt-based sauce.

INGREDIENTS

- 1 (3-ounce) package ramen noodles, chili flavor
- 2 (6-ounce) cans salmon, drained
- 1 tablespoon all-purpose flour
- 2 tablespoons mayonnaise
- 1 large egg, lightly beaten
- 1 tablespoon chopped fresh cilantro
- 1 scallion, minced
- 2 tablespoons vegetable or canola oil
- ½ cup plain yogurt

1. Break the ramen noodles into the bowl of a food processor and pulse until they resemble fine bread crumbs (reserve the ramen seasoning).

2. In a bowl, combine the salmon, flour, mayonnaise, egg, cilantro, scallion, and 3 tablespoons of the ground ramen. Using your hands, form the salmon mixture into four patties. Place the patties on a plate, cover them with plastic wrap, and refrigerate for 30 minutes to allow them to firm up.

3. Meanwhile, put the remaining ground ramen noodles in a shallow bowl or pie plate, sprinkle in about ½ teaspoon of the ramen seasoning, and stir to combine.

4. When the salmon patties are cold and firm, remove them from the refrigerator and dredge each patty in the seasoned ground ramen.

5. In a large nonstick skillet over medium-high heat, heat the oil. When the oil is hot enough that it sizzles, add the croquettes and cook until browned, about 9 minutes on each side.

6. In a small bowl, stir together the yogurt with the remaining ramen seasoning. Serve the sauce with the croquettes.

SALMON AND BOK CHOY IN PARCHMENT

SERVES 4

Food cooked in parchment (or en papillote, as the French say) is always a statement: A sealed parchment package is set before the diner, and as the package is opened, a puff of fragrant steam gives a hint to the delicious food waiting inside. You can also cook this meal in pieces of aluminum foil. Foil is easier to work with since it holds its shape better when you crimp it, but the presentation isn't as pretty.

INGREDIENTS

1 (3-ounce) package ramen noodles, any flavor
2 tablespoons soy sauce
1 tablespoon fresh lime juice
1 teaspoon grated fresh ginger
½ teaspoon sesame oil
2 heads baby bok choy, leaves separated
4 (4 to 6-ounce) salmon fillets

1. Preheat the oven to 400°F. Fold four 12-inch squares of parchment paper in half (Figure 1) and cut one-half of a heart in each (Figure 2). Set aside.

2. Cook the ramen noodles in boiling water for 3 minutes, or according to the package directions (discard the ramen seasoning). Drain and set aside.

3. While the noodles are cooking, in a small bowl, whisk together the soy sauce, lime juice, ginger, and sesame oil and set aside.

4. On one side of each piece of parchment, and leaving at least a 1-inch border, layer the noodles, a few leaves of bok choy (folding the leaves in half if needed), and a salmon fillet (Figure 3). Drizzle about 1 tablespoon sauce over each salmon fillet. To seal the parchment, fold it over the filling and, beginning with the top of the heart, make little overlapping folds to crimp the parchment (Figure 4). When you get to the pointed end, tuck the folded edge of the parchment underneath the package (Figure 5).

5. Place the four packages on a rimmed baking sheet and bake for 15 minutes.

6. To serve, place a closed parchment package (Figure 6) on each plate and allow guests to open it themselves to reveal their meal.

- continued -

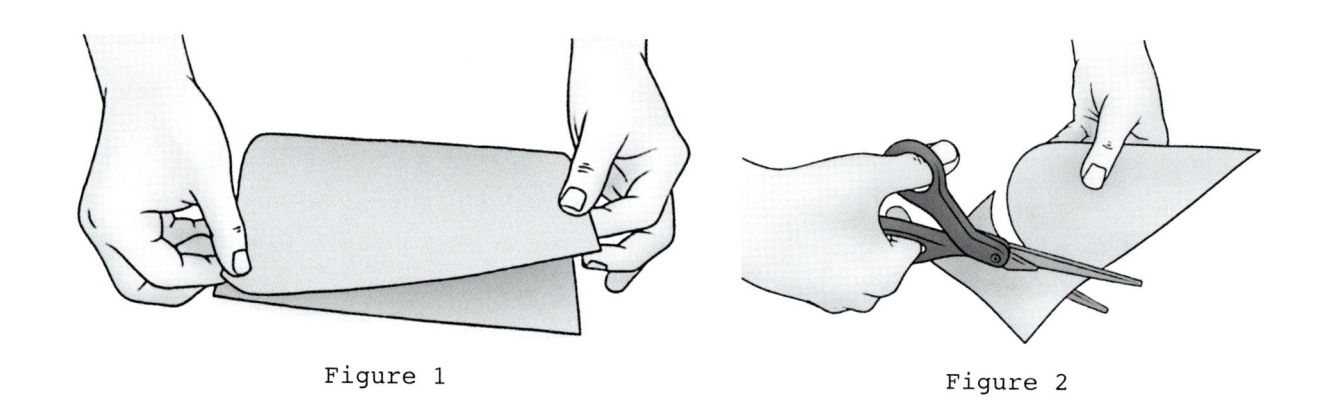

Figure 1

Figure 2

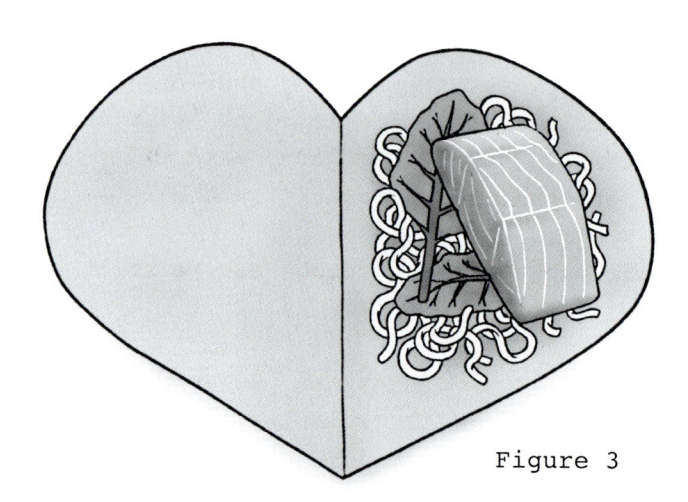

Figure 3

128

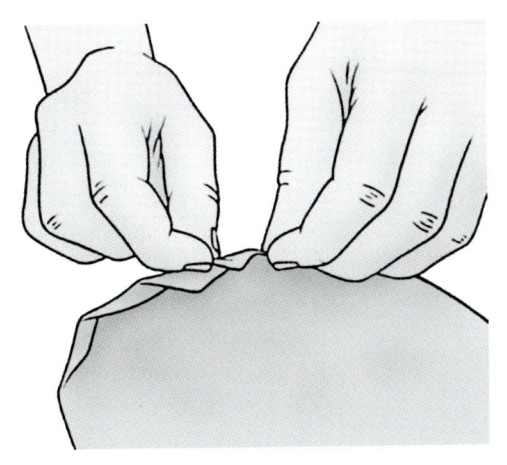

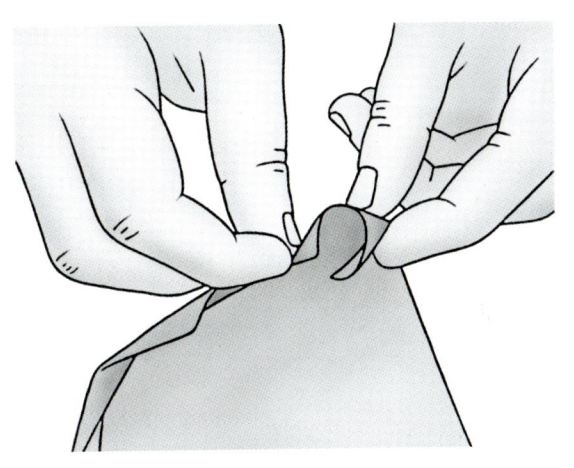

Figure 4

Figure 5

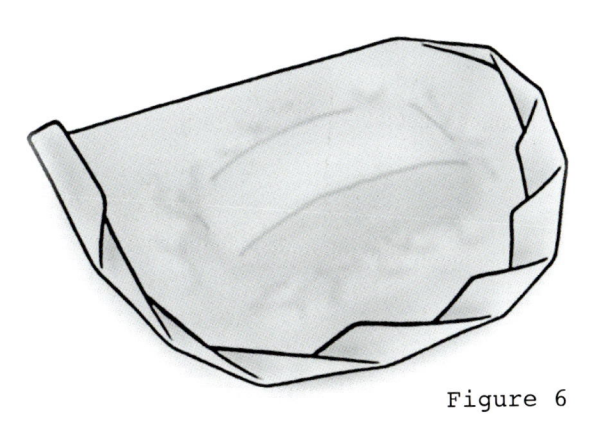

Figure 6

RAMEN RED

SERVES 8

My husband's family has a favorite dish they call spaghetti red. It's basically chili served on a bed of spaghetti noodles. I'm sure it was originally intended as a way for his mother to stretch out leftover chili so that it could make another meal for their family of six, but my husband likes the dish so much that he often asks for spaghetti noodles to go with his chili, even if we haven't reached the leftovers stage yet. Thus, ramen red was born. When you're making a big pot of chili to feed a passel of people, boiling up a few packages of ramen noodles is a way to make this dish more substantial and for the chili to go a little further. Don't forget all the chili fixings—shredded cheese, sour cream, chopped scallions, and black olives are my family's favorites.

INGREDIENTS

- 2 tablespoons vegetable or canola oil
- 2 medium onions, chopped
- 2 cloves garlic, minced
- 1 pound ground turkey or beef, or 1 (16-ounce) package frozen meatless crumbles, like MorningStar Farms
- 2 (28-ounce) cans crushed tomatoes
- 2 (16-ounce) cans kidney beans, drained and rinsed
- 1 (16-ounce) can black beans, drained and rinsed
- 1 (6-ounce) can tomato paste
- 1 tablespoon ground cumin
- 4 (3-ounce) packages ramen noodles, chili flavor

1 teaspoon chili powder,
  medium heat, or more to taste
Salt and pepper

TOPPINGS
Shredded Colby cheese
Chopped scallions
Sliced black olives
Sour cream
Lime wedges
Chopped fresh cilantro

1. In a large saucepan over medium-high heat or Dutch oven, heat the oil. Add the onions and sauté, stirring occasionally, until they're softened and translucent, about 5 minutes. Add the garlic and cook, stirring constantly, for 30 seconds.

2. Add the turkey or beef and cook, breaking up chunks with a spoon, until the meat is browned and cooked through, about 7 minutes. Use a spoon to remove any excess fat or liquid, then add the tomatoes, kidney and black beans, and tomato paste and stir to combine. Bring to a simmer and stir in the cumin, 1 packet ramen seasoning (discard the remainder), and chile powder. Season to taste with salt and pepper. Simmer until heated through and the flavors have had a chance to meld, 10 to 15 minutes.

3. Break the ramen noodles into large pieces and cook them in a large pot of boiling water for 3 minutes. Drain.

4. To serve, place the noodles in shallow bowls and spoon the chili over the top. Allow guests to top their chili with the toppings of their choice.

RAMEN MARY

SERVES 8 TO 10

My friend Adam, who tended bar at a place I used to frequent in Brooklyn, makes the best Bloody Mary I've ever had. So when I had the idea that the unused seasoning packets from a package of ramen would nicely flavor a batch of Bloody Mary mix, I knew just the right person to ask about it. Adam rose to the occasion, developing a fantastic mix that is the perfect thing to serve at a brunch or the next time you have friends over to watch a big sports match.

INGREDIENTS

2 quarts tomato juice
4 ounces prepared horseradish (not cream style)
Juice of 1½ lemons
Juice of 2½ limes
2 tablespoons Worcestershire sauce
1 beef flavor ramen seasoning packet
2 teaspoons cracked black pepper (or to taste)
½ teaspoon salt or celery salt (or to taste)

1 teaspoon Tabasco sauce (or to taste; chipotle Tabasco will add smokiness and depth)
Vodka

GARNISHES
Lemon and lime wedges
Celery sticks
Pickled green beans
Olives
Large boiled shrimp

1. In a pitcher, stir together the tomato juice, horseradish, lemon juice, lime juice, Worcestershire sauce, and ramen seasoning. Season to taste with pepper, salt, and Tabasco sauce. Refrigerate until needed.

2. To prepare a drink, fill a pint glass with ice, add 2 ounces vodka, and fill the rest of the glass with Bloody Mary mix. Stir to combine. Top with the garnishes of your choice.

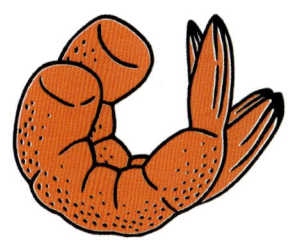

Ramen noodles as dessert? Sure! This assortment of treats uses ramen noodles in unconventional ways to add crunchy or chewy texture to a variety of cakes, cookies, candies, and more. You'll be surprised at how well ramen works in sweets.

Desserts and Sweets

RAMEN-MALLOW CRISPY TREATS

MAKES 4 SQUARES

Did you know those ubiquitous confections made with crisped rice cereal can be made with dry ramen noodles to produce results that are equally delicious? A package of ramen is just enough to make four squares, the perfect-size batch for one or two people. If you don't have a baking dish small enough (4 or 5 inches square is ideal), you could use a plastic sandwich-size food-storage container, or just shape them free-form.

INGREDIENTS

1 (3-ounce) package ramen noodles, any flavor
1 tablespoon unsalted butter, plus more for preparing the pan
1½ cups mini marshmallows
Pinch of salt

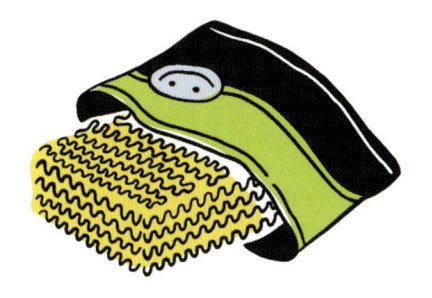

1. Butter a small (about 5-inch square) baking pan or heatproof plastic container.

2. Crumble the ramen noodles into a medium bowl (discard the ramen seasoning).

3. In a small saucepan over low heat, melt the butter. Add the marshmallows and stir frequently, until they are smooth and completely melted. Remove from the heat, add the crumbled ramen noodles and salt, and stir to coat the noodles completely with the marshmallow mixture.

4. Press the mixture into the prepared container, making sure it is an even thickness. Allow to cool completely before cutting.

CANDIED RAMEN SPRINKLE

MAKES ¾ CUP

This versatile topping adds sweet crunch to ice cream, yogurt, baked goods, and fruit salad. If you're making this on the stove, be sure to stir it often and watch it carefully—it can easily scorch.

INGREDIENTS

1 (3-ounce) package ramen noodles, any flavor
1 tablespoon unsalted butter
2 tablespoons brown sugar
¼ teaspoon ground cinnamon

STOVETOP DIRECTIONS: Crumble the ramen noodles into a medium bowl (discard the ramen seasoning). In a medium nonstick skillet over medium heat, melt the butter. Add the brown sugar and cinnamon and stir until the sugar melts and the mixture is syrupy. Add the ramen, stirring to coat it with the sugar mixture, and cook, stirring frequently, until the ramen begins to brown and the sugar mixture looks dry, about 5 minutes. Spread the noodles on a plate and let cool. They will keep for 4 to 5 days at room temperature in a sealed container or zip-top bag.

OVEN DIRECTIONS: Preheat the oven to 350°F. Line a rimmed baking sheet with parchment paper. Crumble the ramen noodles into a medium bowl (discard the ramen seasoning). Melt the butter in the microwave. Drizzle the butter over the ramen and stir to combine. Stir in the brown sugar and cinnamon. Spread the ramen on the prepared baking sheet and bake until the ramen begins to brown and the sugar mixture looks dry, 5 to 8 minutes, stirring once halfway through cooking. Cool and store the noodles as above.

CHOCOLATE PEANUT HAYSTACKS

MAKES 1 DOZEN HAYSTACKS

Next time you're asked to bring a treat to a party or a meeting, whip up a batch or two of these haystack candies. They're easy to make and require only four ingredients, ones that you probably have in your cupboard already.

INGREDIENTS

½ cup semisweet chocolate chips
2 tablespoons smooth peanut butter
1 (3-ounce) package ramen noodles, any flavor
½ cup roasted shelled peanuts

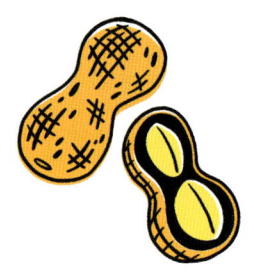

1. Line a rimmed baking sheet with parchment paper.

2. In a double boiler or in the microwave, melt the chocolate chips, stirring until the chocolate is smooth. Stir in the peanut butter.

3. Crumble the ramen noodles into a medium bowl and add the peanuts (discard the ramen seasoning). Stir in the chocolate mixture, coating the ramen and nuts completely.

4. Drop the mixture by the spoonful onto the prepared baking sheet.

5. Refrigerate until firm, 1 to 2 hours, or overnight. Keep refrigerated or store in a cool place.

RAMEN NOODLE PUDDING

SERVES 4 TO 6

This recipe is inspired by my grandmother's noodle kugel, a traditional dish that she served for the Jewish new year. Typically, kugel is made with wide egg noodles, but in this version, the pudding is less dense and has a creamier consistency.

INGREDIENTS

3 large eggs
⅔ cup sugar
½ cup sour cream
½ cup applesauce
2 teaspoons ground cinnamon
½ teaspoon ground ginger
2 (3-ounce) packages ramen noodles, any flavor
5 tablespoons unsalted butter, diced
½ cup raisins

1. Preheat the oven to 350°F. Butter an 8-inch square) glass or metal baking dish.

2. In a large bowl, whisk the eggs, then add the sugar, sour cream, applesauce, cinnamon, and ginger, and whisk to combine.

3. Cook the ramen noodles in boiling water for 2½ minutes (discard the ramen seasoning). Drain the noodles, return to the pot, and toss with the butter until the butter is completely melted. Add the noodle mixture to the egg mixture and stir to completely coat the noodles. Stir in the raisins.

4. Transfer the combined mixture to the prepared baking dish. Bake until the pudding is set and no longer jiggly, 45 minutes to 1 hour.

5. Serve warm, at room temperature, or chilled. The noodle pudding will keep for 3 to 4 days covered in the refrigerator.

COCONUT-LIME BARS

MAKES 16 BARS

Lemon or lime bars are one of my favorite bakery treats, so I was excited when my friend Kelley dreamed up a version that had a crust made of coconut and crushed ramen. Sprinkled with more toasted coconut on top, these bars are the perfect balance of tangy and sweet.

INGREDIENTS

1 (3-ounce) package ramen noodles, any flavor

½ cup plus 2 tablespoons all-purpose flour, divided

¾ cup confectioners' sugar, divided

1 cup sweetened shredded coconut, divided

2 tablespoons grated lime zest, divided

½ teaspoon salt

4 tablespoons unsalted butter, cut into small cubes

¼ cup ice water

4 large eggs

1⅓ cups granulated sugar

1 teaspoon baking powder

½ cup lime juice (from 4 to 5 limes)

1. Preheat the oven to 350°F. Butter a 9-inch square baking dish.

2. Break the ramen noodles into the bowl of a food processor and pulse until they resemble fine bread crumbs (discard the ramen seasoning). Add ½ cup of the flour, ½ cup of the confectioners' sugar, ½ cup of the shredded coconut, 1 tablespoon of the lime zest, and the salt and

pulse about ten times to combine. Add the butter to the bowl and pulse about ten more times to combine. Add half of the water and pulse a few times to combine. Add the remaining water and pulse until the dough forms a large ball, about ten pulses. Scrape the sides of the food processor to add the remaining dough to the ball.

3. Place the dough in the prepared baking dish. Use your hands to press the dough into the bottom and a ¼ inch up the sides of the baking dish. Bake until lightly golden, about 20 minutes.

4. While the dough is baking, beat the eggs in a large bowl. Add the granulated sugar, the remaining 2 tablespoons flour, the baking powder, lime juice, and the remaining 1 tablespoon lime zest. Whisk until completely combined.

5. Remove the crust from the oven and lower the heat to 325°F. Whisk the egg mixture again to recombine and pour it over the dough. Bake the bars until the filling is set and looks dry on the top, about 25 minutes. Remove from the oven and let cool on a wire rack.

6. Spread the remaining ¼ cup coconut on a rimmed baking sheet and bake at 325°F until lightly toasted, about 10 minutes. Remove from the oven and let cool.

7. Using a fine-mesh strainer, sift the remaining ¼ cup confectioners' sugar over the top of the lime bars to coat lightly. Sprinkle the top with the toasted coconut. Cool completely before cutting into squares.

TROPICAL FRUIT SALAD WITH CRISPY RAMEN-COCONUT TOPPING

SERVES 8 TO 12

This creamy, coconutty fruit salad is one of my mother's go-to recipes for summer parties or afternoon teas, although the crispy ramen and toasted coconut topping is my own twist. You can use any combination of fruit, but I love to include mandarin oranges and canned pineapple. The oranges add a fancy touch, and the pineapple is such a nice tropical complement to the coconut. This salad will get watery and the ramen topping will get soggy if it sits too long before serving. If you're transporting it or you're not going to serve it right away, make and store the components (fruit, dressing, and topping) separately. Just before serving, drain any excess juice from the fruit mixture, stir the yogurt dressing into the salad, and sprinkle it with the ramen topping.

INGREDIENTS

- 1 (3-ounce) package ramen noodles, any flavor
- 1 tablespoon unsalted butter
- 1 tablespoon brown sugar
- 1 cup sweetened shredded coconut, divided

1 (20-ounce) can pineapple chunks, drained
1 (15-ounce) can mandarin oranges, drained
1 cup grape halves
1 cup sliced strawberries (about half a pint or 6 ounces)
1½ cups cantaloupe chunks (from 1 cantaloupe)
6 ounces low-fat vanilla yogurt
½ teaspoon minced or grated fresh ginger

1. Line a rimmed baking sheet with parchment paper.

2. In a small bowl, crush the ramen noodles with your hands into tiny pieces (discard the ramen seasoning).

3. In a medium nonstick skillet over medium heat, melt the butter and brown sugar, stirring with a wooden spoon until the brown sugar is dissolved completely and the mixture is syrupy. Add the crushed ramen noodles and ½ cup of the coconut and cook, stirring constantly, until the coconut turns golden brown, 2 to 3 minutes. Watch the mixture carefully to keep the coconut from getting too dark or burning. Spread the ramen mixture on the prepared baking sheet to cool.

4. In a serving bowl, combine the pineapple, mandarin oranges, grapes, strawberries, and cantaloupe. In a small bowl, stir together the yogurt, the remaining ½ cup coconut, and the ginger. Stir to combine. Stir the yogurt dressing into the fruit salad, mixing well to coat the fruit completely. Just before serving, sprinkle the salad with the crispy ramen topping. Serve immediately.

TWO BASIC RECIPES

HOW TO POACH CHICKEN

Poaching is a great method to achieve tender, moist chicken meat. Use poached chicken to make chicken salad, such as Chinese Chicken Salad (page 66), or in sandwiches.

1. Place a chicken in a small pot or deep saucepan. Cover the chicken with chicken broth, enough to completely submerge the chicken. Bring to a boil over high heat, then lower the heat, cover, and simmer until the chicken is cooked through, about 30 minutes. The chicken's internal temperature should measure 165°F on a meat thermometer.

2. Remove the chicken from the broth and let it cool until it's no longer too hot to handle. Use a knife to slice off the breasts and the legs and use your fingers to remove and discard the skin and pull the meat off the bones. Use a knife to chop the chicken according to the recipe instructions.

3. The cooled chicken broth can be skimmed of excess fat and reserved to use in any recipe that calls for chicken broth or stock.

PARMESAN RAMEN CROUTONS   MAKES 8 TO 12 CROUTONS

Use the crunchy cake of dry ramen noodles in place of bread to make an unusual crouton that's perfect on a salad, such as Caesar Salad with Parmesan Ramen Croutons (page 60) or floating atop a bowl of soup, like Tomato Soup with Parmesan Ramen Croutons (page 54). Actually, it's hard not to just eat these croutons on their own.

INGREDIENTS

- ½ teaspoon garlic powder
- 1 tablespoon grated Parmesan cheese
- 1 package ramen noodles, any flavor
- 2 tablespoons unsalted butter, melted, divided

- continued -

1. Preheat a toaster oven or conventional oven to 350°F and line a rimmed baking sheet with parchment paper.

2. In a small bowl, stir together the garlic powder and Parmesan cheese.

3. Carefully break apart the two layers of the ramen cake (discard the ramen seasoning). Then break each half into 4 to 6 large pieces. Arrange the pieces on the prepared baking sheet and brush them with 1 tablespoon of the melted butter. Sprinkle half of the Parmesan mixture over the cakes.

4. Bake for 5 minutes. Remove from the oven, turn each crouton over with a pair of tongs or a spatula, and brush them with the remaining 1 tablespoon butter and sprinkle with the rest of the Parmesan mixture. Bake until the croutons are lightly browned, about 5 minutes longer.

CONVERSIONS

MEASURE	EQUIVALENT	METRIC
1 teaspoon	--	5 milliliters
1 tablespoon	3 teaspoons	14.8 milliliters
1 cup	16 tablespoons	236.8 milliliters
1 pint	2 cups	473.6 milliliters
1 quart	4 cups	947.2 milliliters
1 liter	4 cups + 3½ tablespoons	1000 milliliters
1 ounce (dry)	2 tablespoons	28.35 grams
1 pound	16 ounces	453.49 grams
2.21 pounds	35.3 ounces	1 kilogram
270°F / 350°F	--	132°C / 177°C

APPENDIX

RAMEN MANUFACTURERS AND RETAILERS

Ramen is so ubiquitous you're likely to find packages even at a gas station or a convenience store. But if you're looking for unusual flavors, want to experiment with different brands, or if you prefer to buy in bulk, here are some of the main manufacturers and online retailers of ramen noodles.

Dr. McDougall's • www.rightfoods.com
The ramen cups from this health food brand are baked, rather than fried, and made with meatless flavorings appropriate for vegetarians. Look for vegan chicken, hot and sour, and other flavors in its ramen line. They'll be found in natural food stores or the health food aisle of the supermarket.

Instant Ramen Shop • instantramenshop.com
This online resource for premium Japanese ramen brands ships worldwide from Japan. The site carries products from Nissin, Ippudo, New Touch, and more, with a wide variety of flavor options.

Koyo • koyonoodles.com
More expensive than most mainstream ramen brands, Koyo uses organic and higher-quality ingredients like heirloom wheat and sea salt and contains no MSG. The products are vegan and come in flavors like shiitake mushroom, wakame seaweed, lemongrass ginger, and garlic pepper. Also, the dry noodles

are baked, rather than flash-fried like most. Look for this brand in natural food stores.

Lotus Foods • lotusfoods.com
Lotus foods makes gluten-free ramen noodles that are suitable to use in the recipes in this book. Noodle options include millet and brown rice, forbidden rice, and jade pearl rice and come with or without soup base mixes. Look for this brand in natural food stores.

Maruchan • maruchan.com
In additional to the traditional flavors of beef, chicken, soy sauce, and shrimp, Maruchan's ramen flavors include picante chicken, lime chili shrimp, roast beef, and creamy chicken. The company's Maruchan Gold line is air-dried and comes in spicy miso or soy sauce flavors. The company also makes low-sodium products.

Momofuku Goods • shop.momofuku.com
An offshoot of the popular New York City restaurant of the same name, this site is a source for top-quality air-dried noodles that come with sauce packs. Flavors include soy and scallion, sweet and spicy, and spicy chili.

My Ramen Box • myramenbox.com
This Korean instant noodle company has been around since the 1960s. Its shin ramyun noodles come in a variety of flavors, including an air-dried version that's lower in fat.

Nissin Foods • nissinfoods.com
Founded by Momofuku Ando, Nissin Foods is the inventor of instant ramen. The company's Top Ramen packaged instant noodles come in chicken, beef, and shrimp flavors, as well as vegetarian flavors that include soy sauce and chili.

Nongshim • nongshimusa.com
This Korean instant noodle company's version of instant ramen noodles is ramyun, and flavors include shin ramyun (which is so spicy it "makes a man cry," according to the company's website), kimchi ramyun, and seafood ramyun. It's sold at many warehouse stores.

Public Goods • publicgoods.com
This company is on the mission to make more sustainable household goods and packaged food products, including ramen noodles that come in a beautifully minimalist package. Flavors include sesame paste, spicy sesame, and soy sauce.

Sun Noodle • sunnoodle.com
Founded in Hawaii, Sun Noodle makes fresh ramen that comes with seasoning packets in flavors like miso and shoyu. This ramen is good for the soup or stir-fry type recipes in this book.

Sugoi Market • sugoi-market.com
On this site you can buy Sapporo Ichiban ramen noodles in a variety of traditional and more interesting flavors, including tonkatsu, shio, and hot and spicy chicken.

SOURCES FOR OTHER INGREDIENTS

Most of the ingredients in this book can be found in your local supermarket, especially if it has a well-stocked Asian foods section. You can also find many ingredients in an Asian grocery store if you have one nearby. But if you have trouble locally, try shopping online at these sites:

Amazon • amazon.com
Ramen by the case, sauces, and seasonings

Asian Food Grocer • asianfoodgrocer.com
Imported ramen, sauce, vinegar, and seasonings, including nori furikake

H Mart • hmart.com
The online version of an Asian supermarket with locations on the East Coast, and in Illinois, Texas, Georgia, and California; ramen noodles, sauces and seasonings, seaweed, nori furikake, and miso paste

Temple of Thai • templeofthai.com
Thai ingredients, including fresh produce, curries, chiles, spices, coconut milk, and Mama Noodles brand ramen noodles

INDEX

A
Ando, Momofuku, 9–10, 15, 154
Asian Chicken Noodle Soup, 48–49
Asparagus, Ramen Alfredo with, 98–99

B
Bacon, Egg, and Noodle Scramble, 36–37
beans
　Green Beans with Crunchy Sesame Ramen Topping, 70–71
　Ramen Red, 130–31
beef
　Beef Stroganoff on Buttered Parsley Ramen Noodles, 106–7
　Cold Noodle Salad with Grilled Beef, 64–65
　Ramen Bolognese, 104–5
　Ramen Red, 130–31
　Spicy Beef and Mushroom Stew, 56–57
　Vietnamese Noodle Soup, 50–51
Bird's Nests with Spinach, Egg, and Cheese, 40–41
Bok Choy in Parchment, Salmon and, 126–29
bread
　Ramen-Crusted Cinnamon French Toast, 42–43
broccoli
　Sesame Chicken and Broccoli, 86–88
　Southern-Style Slaw, 68–69

C
cabbage
　Southern-Style Slaw, 68–69
Caesar Salad with Parmesan Ramen Croutons, 60–61
cheese
　Bird's Nests with Spinach, Egg, and Cheese, 40–41
　Kale-Cheddar Noodle Casserole, 108–9
　Parmesan Ramen Croutons, 149–50
　Ramen Alfredo with Asparagus, 98–99
　Ramen-n-Cheese, 62–63
　Ramen Pan Pizza, 24–25
　Ramen with Cherry Tomatoes and Mozzarella, 74–75
　Spaetzle-Style Ramen Noodles, 72–73
　Tuna Noodle Casserole, 121–23
　Zucchini Boats Filled with Ramen and Mushrooms, 110–11
chicken
　Asian Chicken Noodle Soup, 48–49
　Chinese Chicken Salad, 66–67
　poaching, 148
　Ramen-Crusted Chicken Fingers with Honey Mustard Sauce, 102–3
　Sesame Chicken and Broccoli, 86–88
　Thai Coconut-Lemongrass Soup, 52–53
Chinese Chicken Salad, 66–67
Chocolate Peanut Haystacks, 140–41
coconut
　Coconut-Lime Bars, 144–45
　Tropical Fruit Salad with Crispy Ramen-Coconut Topping, 146–47
coconut milk, 13
　Green Coconut Curry Shrimp Bowl, 90–91
　Stir-Fried Vegetables in Coconut Ginger Sauce, 94–95
　Thai Coconut-Lemongrass Soup, 52–53
Croutons, Parmesan Ramen, 149–50
curry paste, 13

D
Dan Dan Noodles, 92–93
desserts, 134
　Candied Ramen Sprinkle, 138–39
　Chocolate Peanut Haystacks, 140–41
　Coconut-Lime Bars, 144–45
　Ramen-Mallow Crispy Treats, 136–37
　Ramen Noodle Pudding, 142–43

Tropical Fruit Salad with Crispy Ramen-Coconut Topping, 146–47
Dip, Creamy Miso, 32–33
drinks
   Ramen Mary, 132–33

E

eggs
   Bacon, Egg, and Noodle Scramble, 36–37
   Bird's Nests with Spinach, Egg, and Cheese, 40–41
   Ramen Brei, 44–45
equipment, 18–19

F

fish. *See* salmon; tuna
fish sauce, 13
French Toast, Ramen-Crusted, 42–43
Fruit Salad, Tropical, with Crispy Ramen-Coconut Topping, 146–47

G

ginger, 13–14

H

Haystacks, Chocolate Peanut, 140–41
hoisin sauce, 14

K

Kale-Cheddar Noodle Casserole, 108–9

M

marshmallows
   Ramen-Mallow Crispy Treats, 136–37
mushrooms
   Beef Stroganoff on Buttered Parsley Ramen Noodles, 106–7
   Spicy Beef and Mushroom Stew, 56–57
   Tuna Noodle Casserole, 121–23
   Zucchini Boats Filled with Ramen and Mushrooms, 110–11

O

oil, 14

P

Pad Thai, 78–79
Pancake, Pan-Fried Scallion, 28–29
party planning, 114–15
peanuts
   Chocolate Peanut Haystacks, 140–41
   Cold Sesame Noodles, 80–81
   Spicy Peanut Noodle Wraps, 30–31
Pizza, Ramen Pan, 24–25
ponzu sauce, 14
pork
   Dan Dan Noodles, 92–93
Pudding, Ramen Noodle, 142–43

R

ramen. *See also individual recipes*
   brands of, 9–10, 12, 13
   buying, 152–54
   consumption of, by country, 20
   cooking, 20
   crushing, 20
   as economic indicator, 12
   grinding, 21
   history of, 9–10, 16
   jazzing up, 11
   manufacture of, 12, 19
   museum for, 10
   in pop culture, 15
   popularity of, 8
rice cooking wine, 15
rice vinegar, 15

S

salads, 58
   Caesar Salad with Parmesan Ramen Croutons, 60–61
   Chinese Chicken Salad, 66–67
   Cold Noodle Salad with Grilled Beef, 64–65
   Tropical Fruit Salad with Crispy Ramen-Coconut Topping, 146–47
salmon
   Salmon and Bok Choy in Parchment, 126–29

Salmon Croquettes with Creamy Chili Sauce, 124–25
seaweed seasoning (nori furikake), 16
sesame oil, 16
sesame seeds, 16
   Sesame Chicken and Broccoli, 86–88
   Sesame-Crusted Tuna with Ponzu Glaze on Ramen Noodles, 84–85
shrimp
   Green Coconut Curry Shrimp Bowl, 90–91
   Loaded Stir-Fry, 82–83
   Tempura Shrimp in Miso-Scallion Soup, 118–20
   Thai Basil Spring Rolls, 26–27
Slaw, Southern-Style, 68–69
soups, 46
   Asian Chicken Noodle Soup, 48–49
   Tempura Shrimp in Miso-Scallion Soup, 118–20
   Thai Coconut-Lemongrass Soup, 52–53
   Tomato Soup with Parmesan Ramen Croutons, 54–55
   Vietnamese Noodle Soup, 50–51
soy sauce, 16
Spaetzle-Style Ramen Noodles, 72–73
Spinach, Bird's Nests with Egg, Cheese, and, 40–41
Spring Rolls, Thai Basil, 26–27

Sprinkle, Candied Ramen, 138–39
Sriracha sauce, 17
stir-fries
   Loaded Stir-Fry, 82–83
   Stir-Fried Vegetables in Coconut Ginger Sauce, 94–95

T

Tempura Shrimp in Miso-Scallion Soup, 118–20
teriyaki sauce, 17
Thai Basil Spring Rolls, 26–27
Thai chili sauce, 17
Thai Coconut-Lemongrass Soup, 52–53
tofu, 17
   Pad Thai, 78–79
   Soy Grilled Tofu on Gingery Noodles, 116–17
   Tempura Shrimp in Miso-Scallion Soup, 118–20
   Thai Basil Spring Rolls, 26–27
tomatoes
   Ramen Bolognese, 104–5
   Ramen Mary, 132–33
   Ramen-Quiles, 38–39
   Ramen Red, 130–31
   Ramen with Cherry Tomatoes and Mozzarella, 74–75
   Tomato Soup with Parmesan Ramen Croutons, 54–55
   Zucchini Boats Filled with Ramen and Mushrooms, 110–11

tuna
   Sesame-Crusted Tuna with Ponzu Glaze on Ramen Noodles, 84–85
   Tuna Noodle Casserole, 121–23
turkey
   Individual Turkey Meat Loaves with Crunchy Ramen Topping, 100–101
   Ramen Bolognese, 104–5
   Ramen Red, 130–31

V

vegetables. *See also individual vegetables*
   Loaded Stir-Fry, 82–83
   Stir-Fried Vegetables in Coconut Ginger Sauce, 94–95
Vietnamese Noodle Soup, 50–51
vodka
   Ramen Mary, 132–33

W

Wraps, Spicy Peanut Noodle, 30–31

Z

Zucchini Boats Filled with Ramen and Mushrooms, 110–11

ACKNOWLEDGMENTS

I am grateful to everyone who came along for the ride on this wonderful adventure of writing my first cookbook—particularly the team at Ulysses Press, who gave me this opportunity and were so pleasant to work with. As I've worked on this special reissued edition many years later, I'm grateful again to the Ulysses team for our longtime collaboration.

A hug to all of my friends in Atlanta, New York, Chicago, and elsewhere who chimed in with ideas, recipes, and encouragement. And a special shout-out to my virtual office mate, Stacie McClintock, who sent me the email that got this whole ball rolling.

A raise of the glass to my good friend Kelley Sparwasser, who let me tap into her endless font of fantastic ideas, and who helped me out with several recipes. And to her husband, Adam Wisniewski, for his wonderful Ramen Mary recipe.

Love to my parents-in-law, Joseph and Christina Harlan, who let me use their kitchen, their babysitting services, and their taste buds on countless occasions. And I am eternally grateful to my brother-in-law Steve Harlan, who's always got my back when it comes to legal matters.

And more love to my own parents, Judy and Greg Goldbogen, my most faithful supporters throughout my life, enthusiastically endorsing my decisions and ideas and championing every accomplishment.

And finally, much love and gratitude to my family. To my husband, Chip Harlan, who is infinitely supportive and proud of me, who eagerly sampled every dish I set before him without ever uttering the words, "Ramen, again?" And to my daughters, Sadie and Gillian, who are thankfully the least picky eaters I know and the best daughters I could possibly have wished for.

ABOUT THE AUTHOR

Jessica Harlan is the author of nine cookbooks, including *Quinoa Cuisine*, *Tortillas to the Rescue*, *Crazy for Breakfast Sandwiches*, and *The Little Book of Takoyaki*. Her food-writing career has taken her to some amazing places: eating a multicourse truffle feast in an Italian village, judging a hot and spicy food competition in Albuquerque, sipping ice cider in Montreal. A graduate of the Institute of Culinary Education, she's written for *HGTV*, *Food Network*, *Southern Living*, *AllRecipes*, *Town & Country*, and more.

She lives in Atlanta with her husband and two teenagers, who never complain when ramen is being served for dinner.

Visit her website at jessicaharlan.com or follow her on Instagram at @jessica_g_harlan.